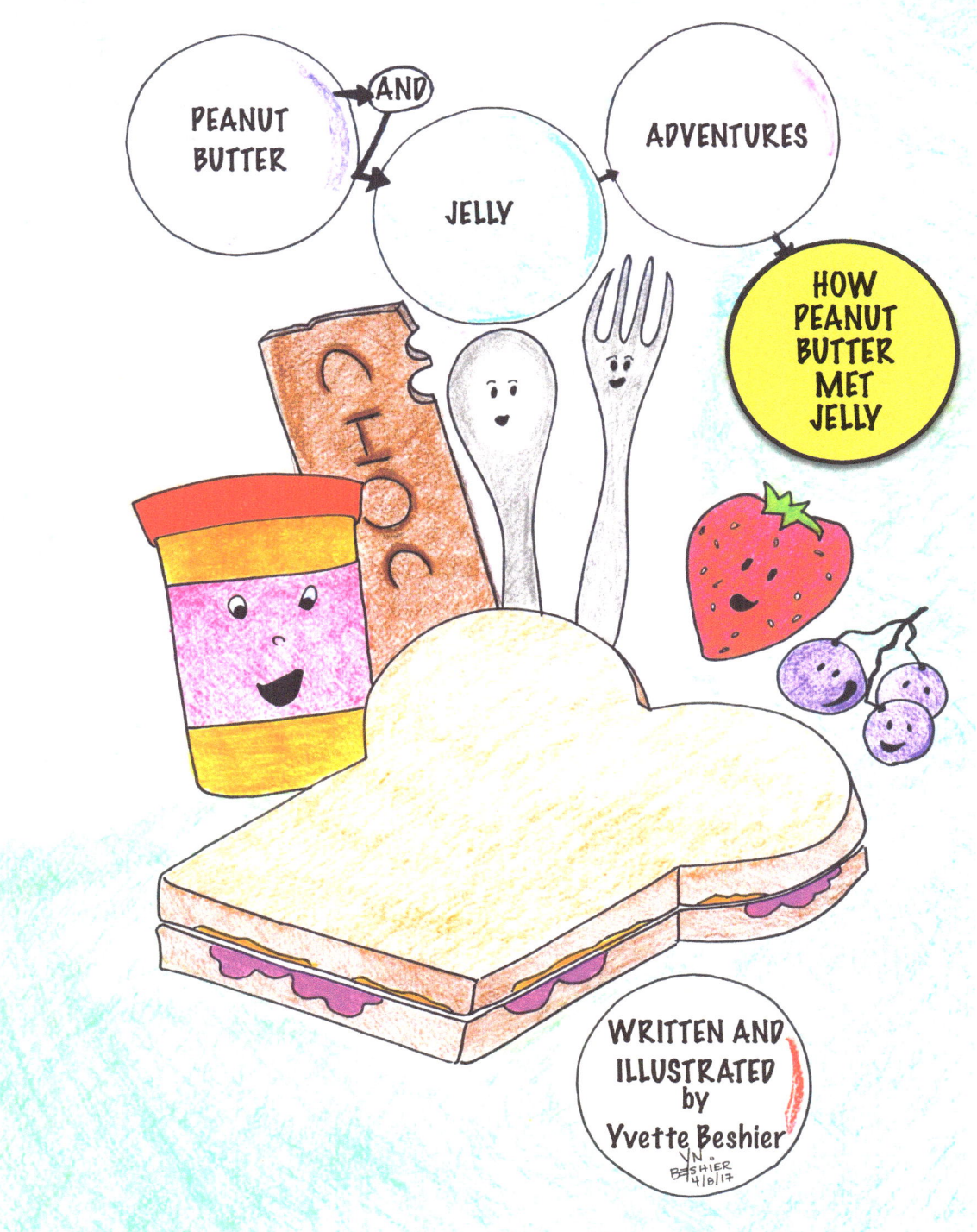

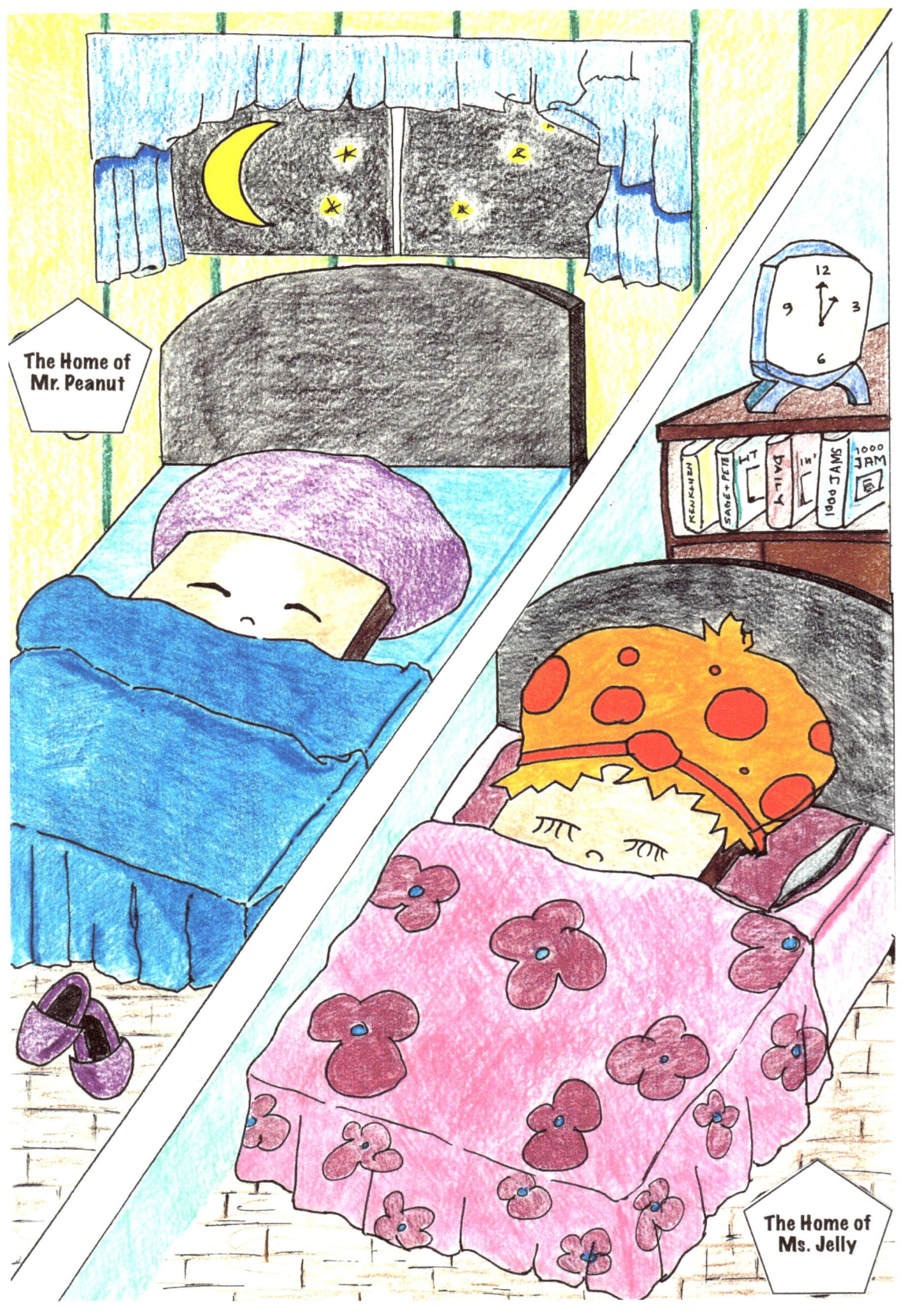

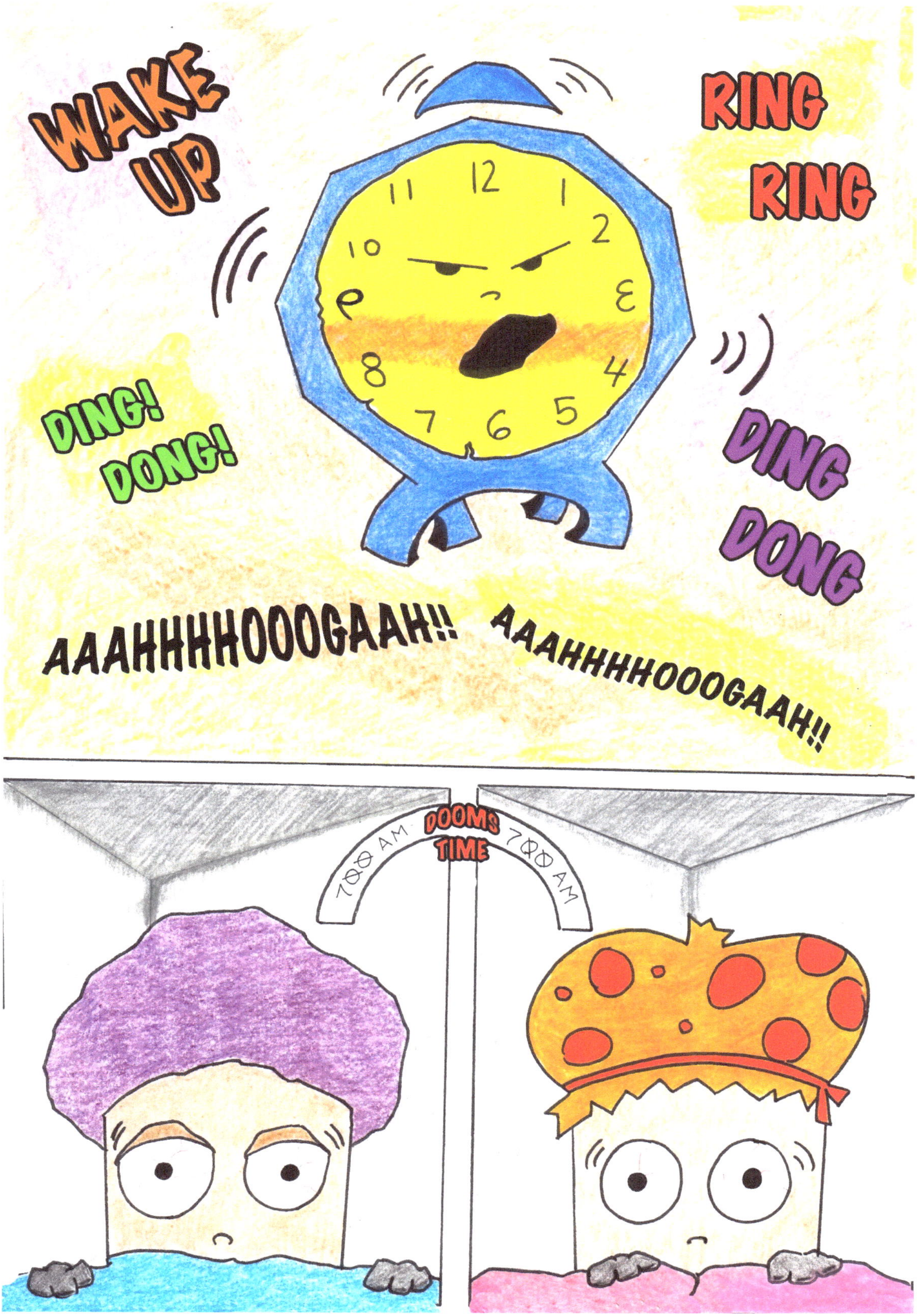

WAKE UP **RING RING**

DING! DONG! **DING DONG**

AAAHHHHOOOGAAH!! **AAAHHHHOOOGAAH!!**

DOOMS TIME

7:00 AM — 7:00 AM

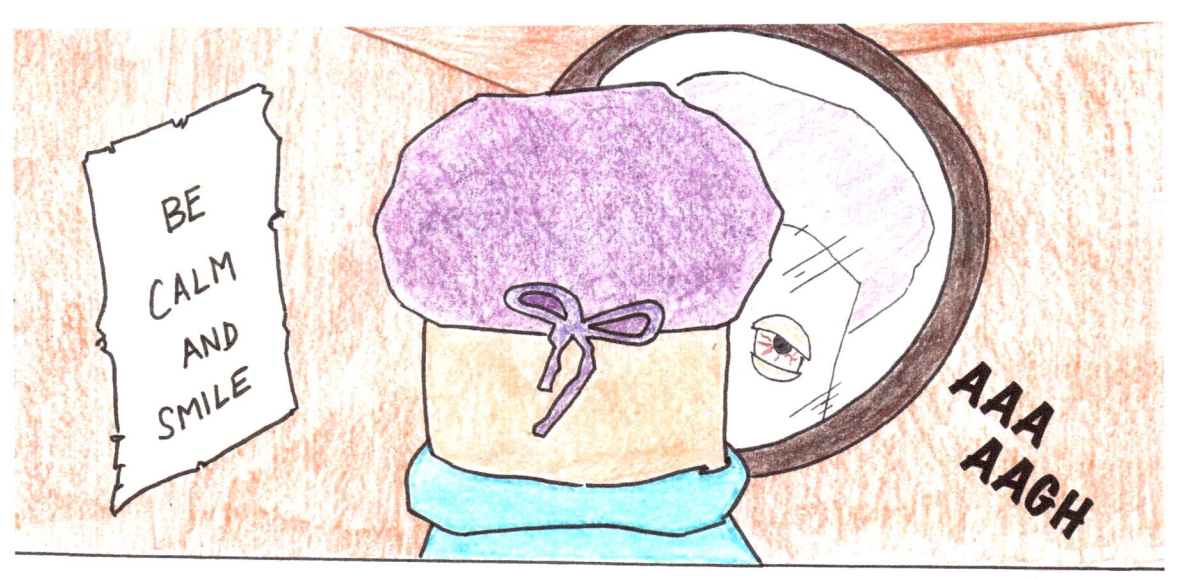
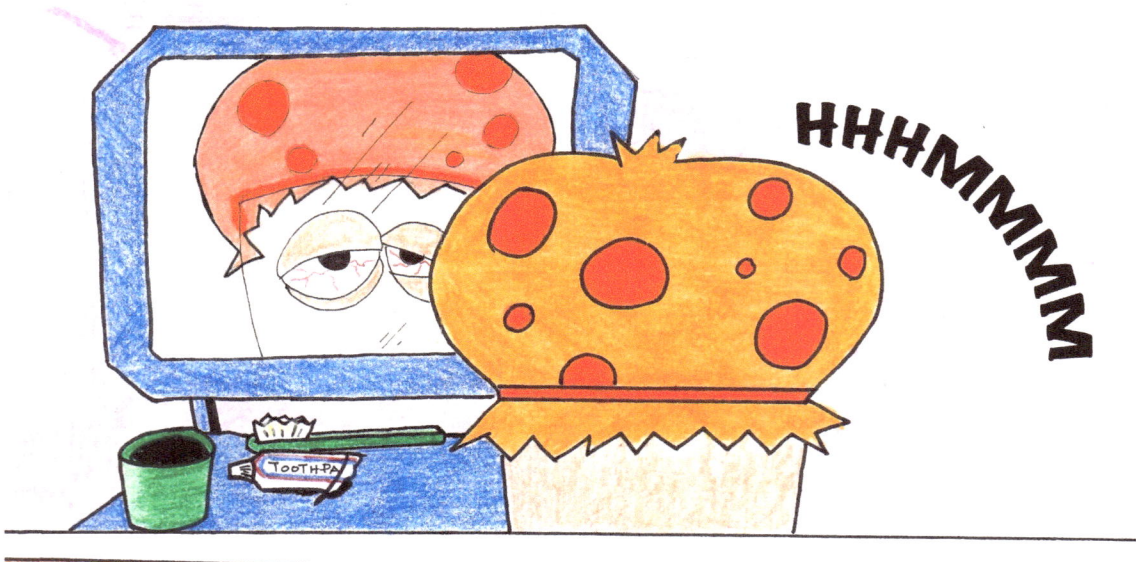
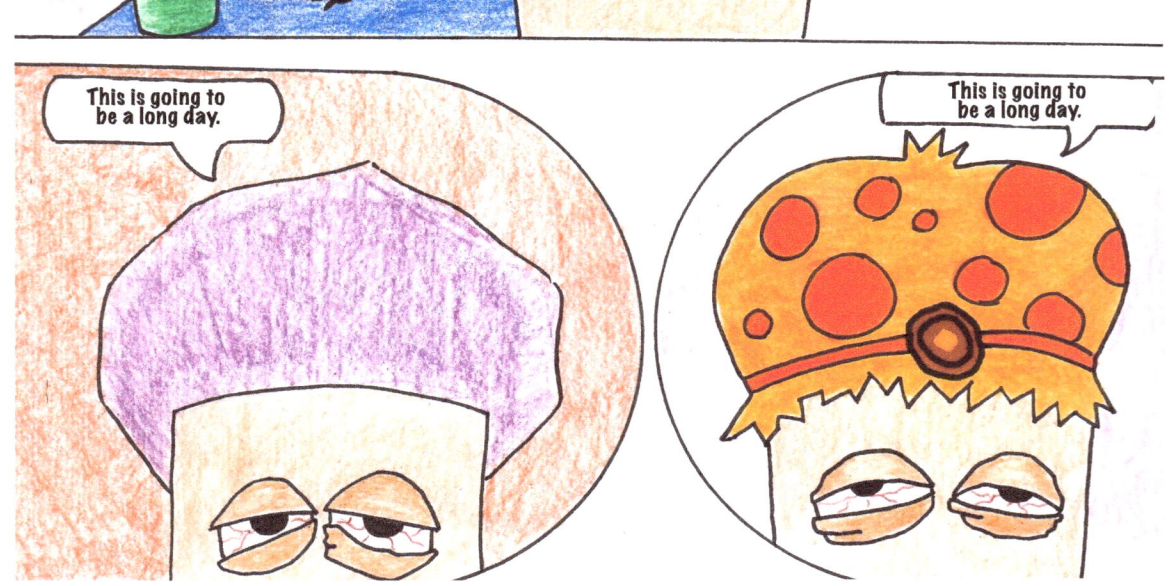

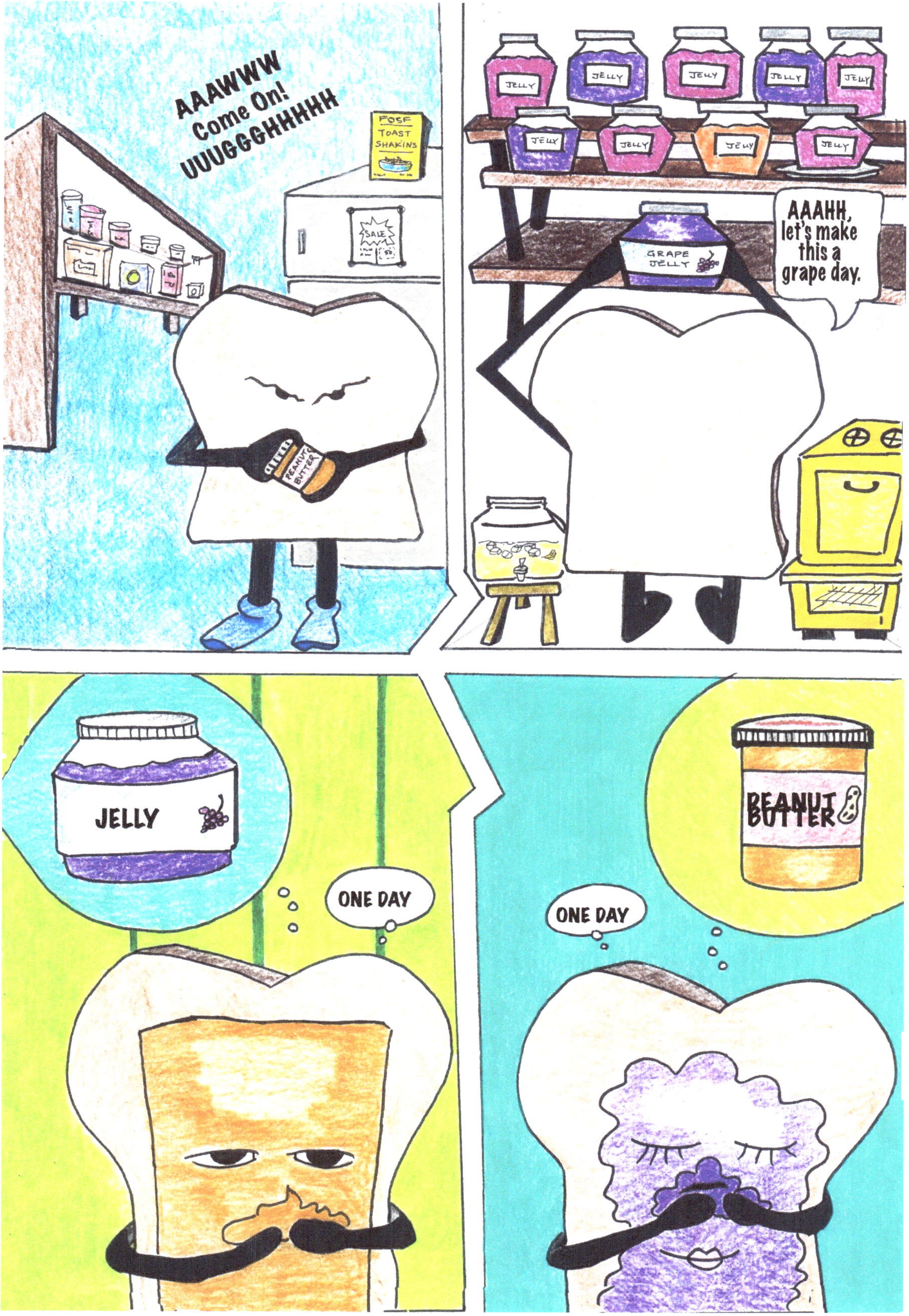

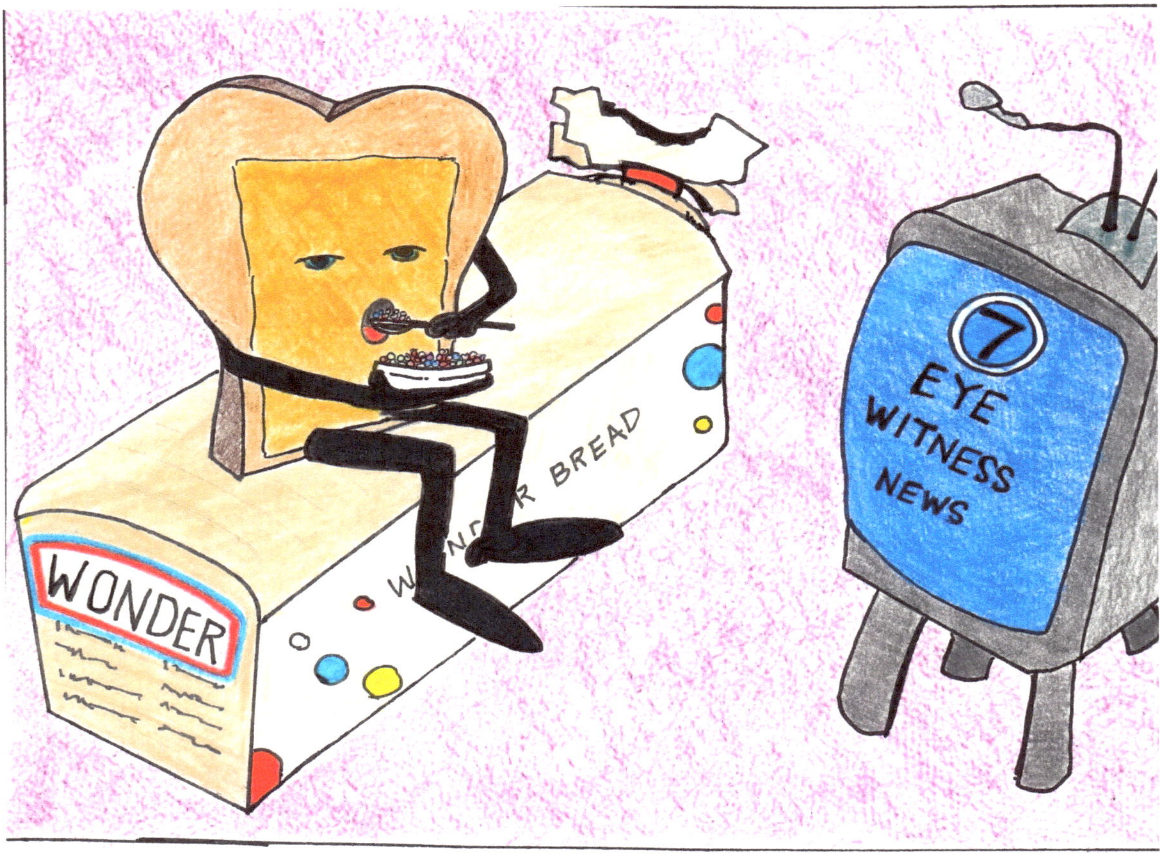

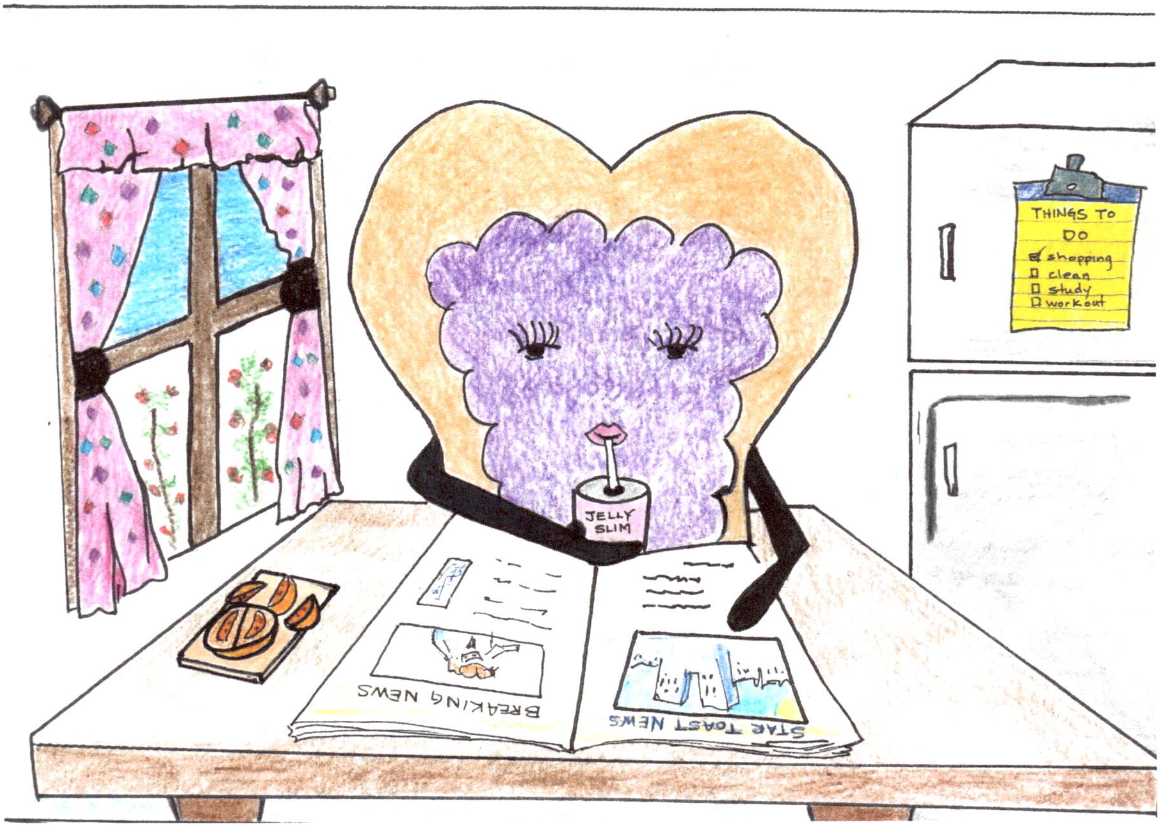

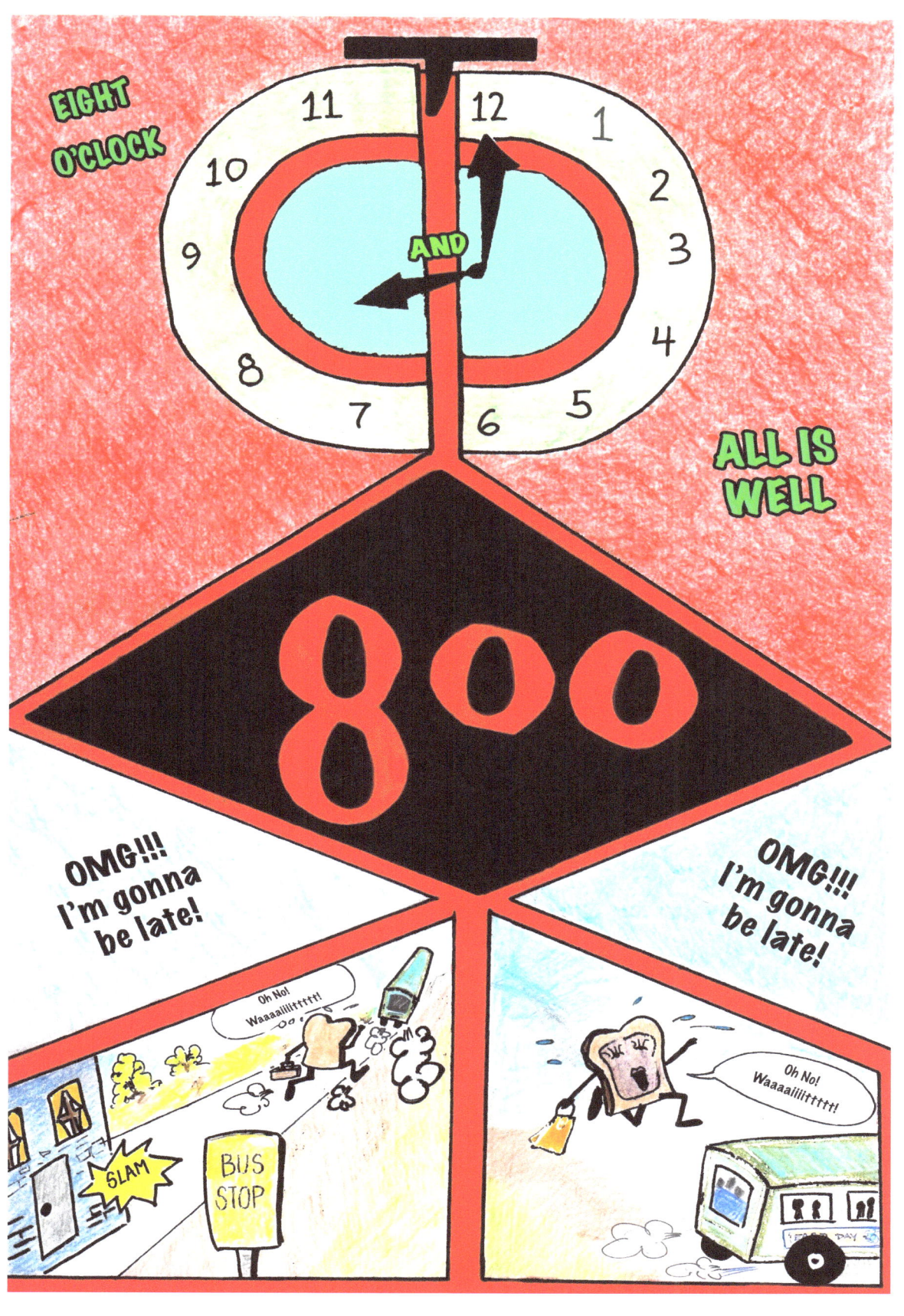

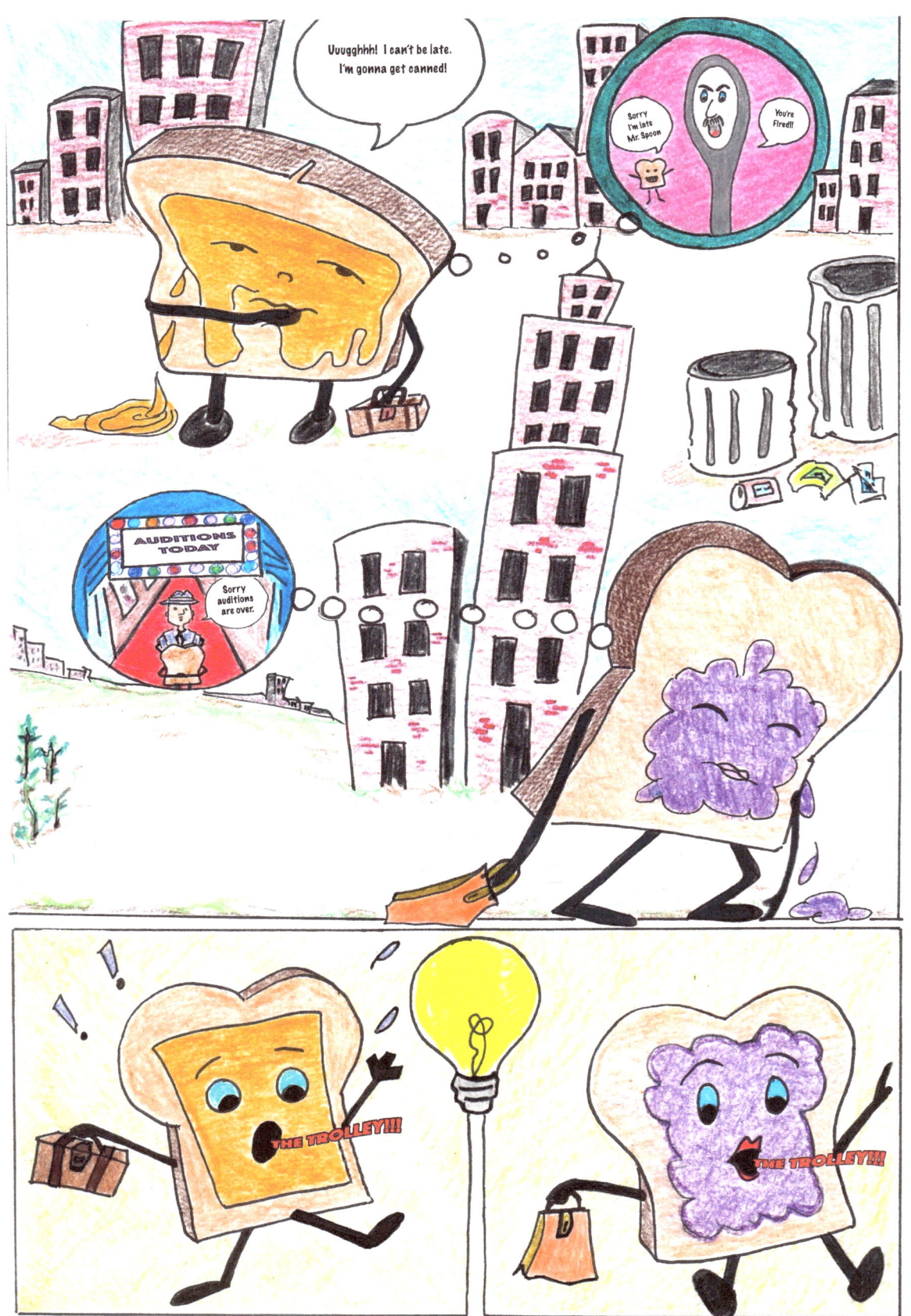

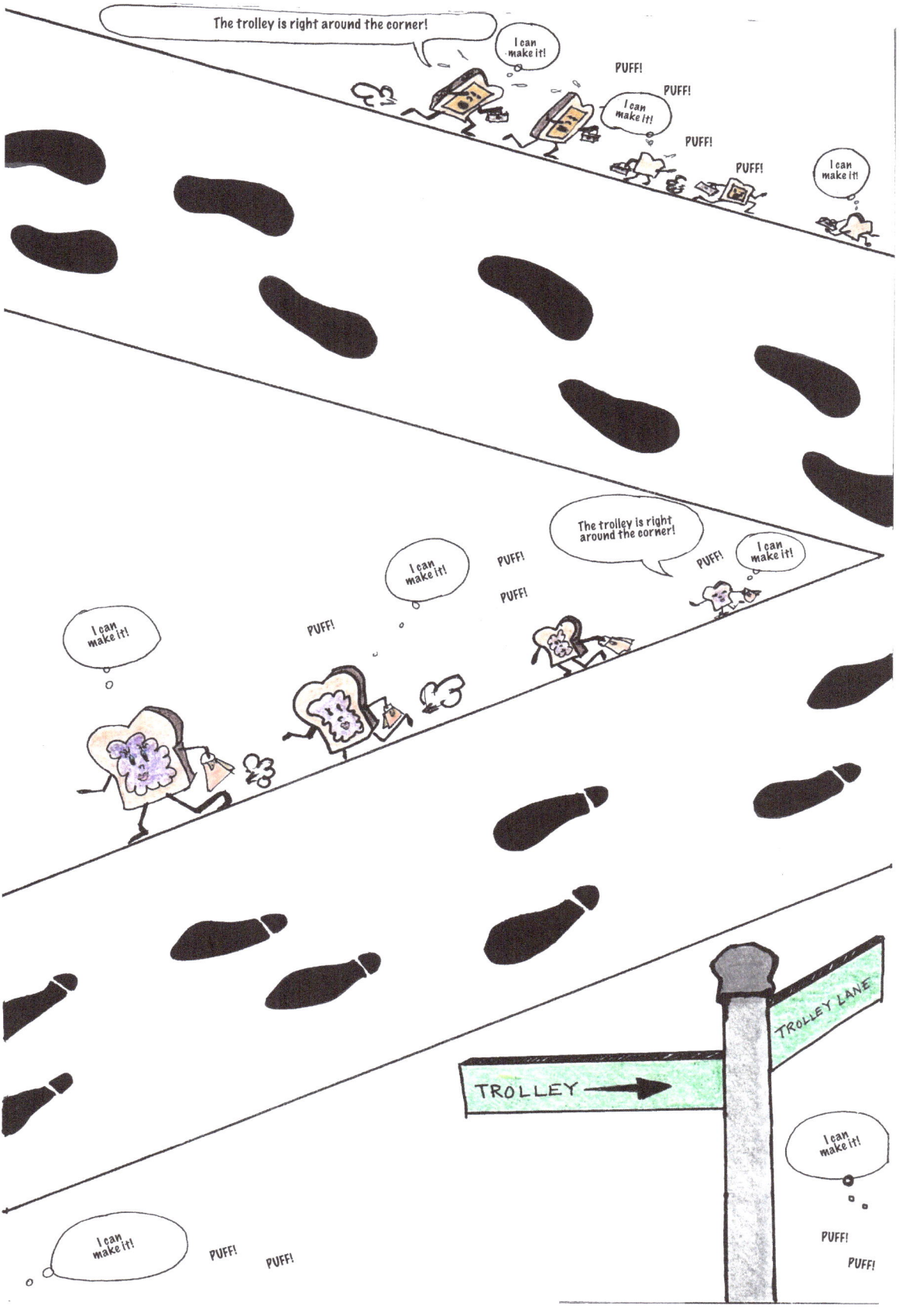

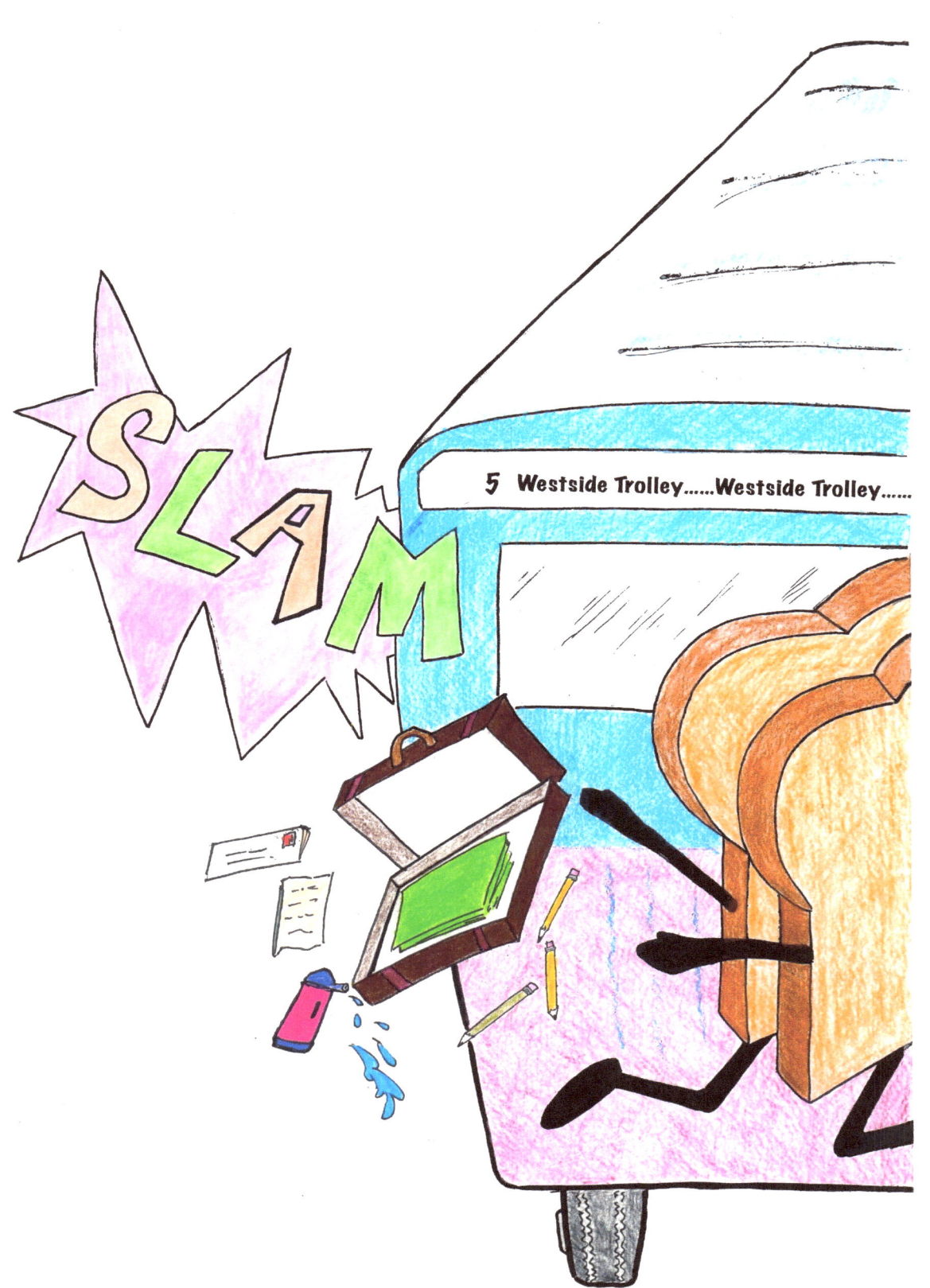

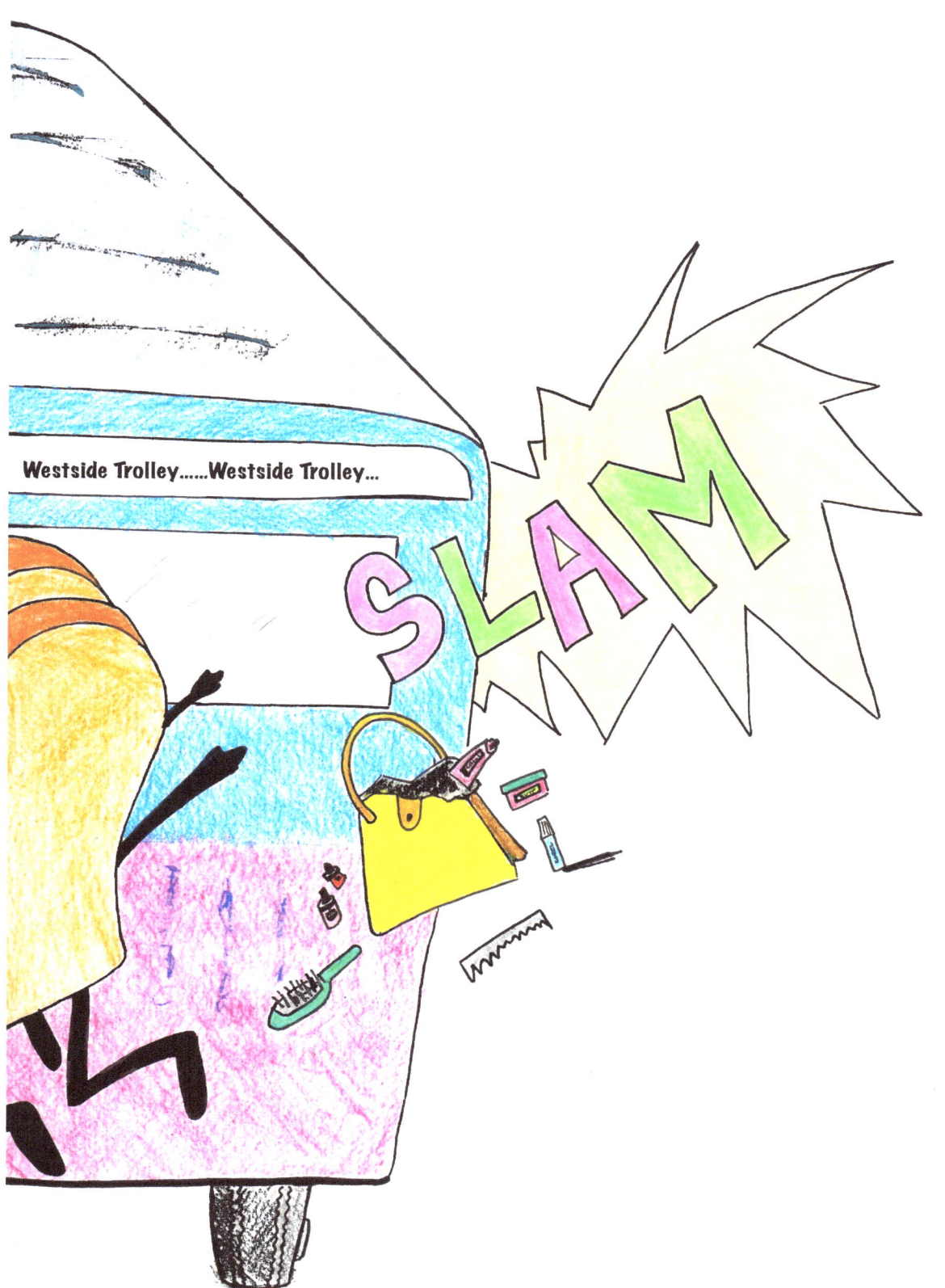

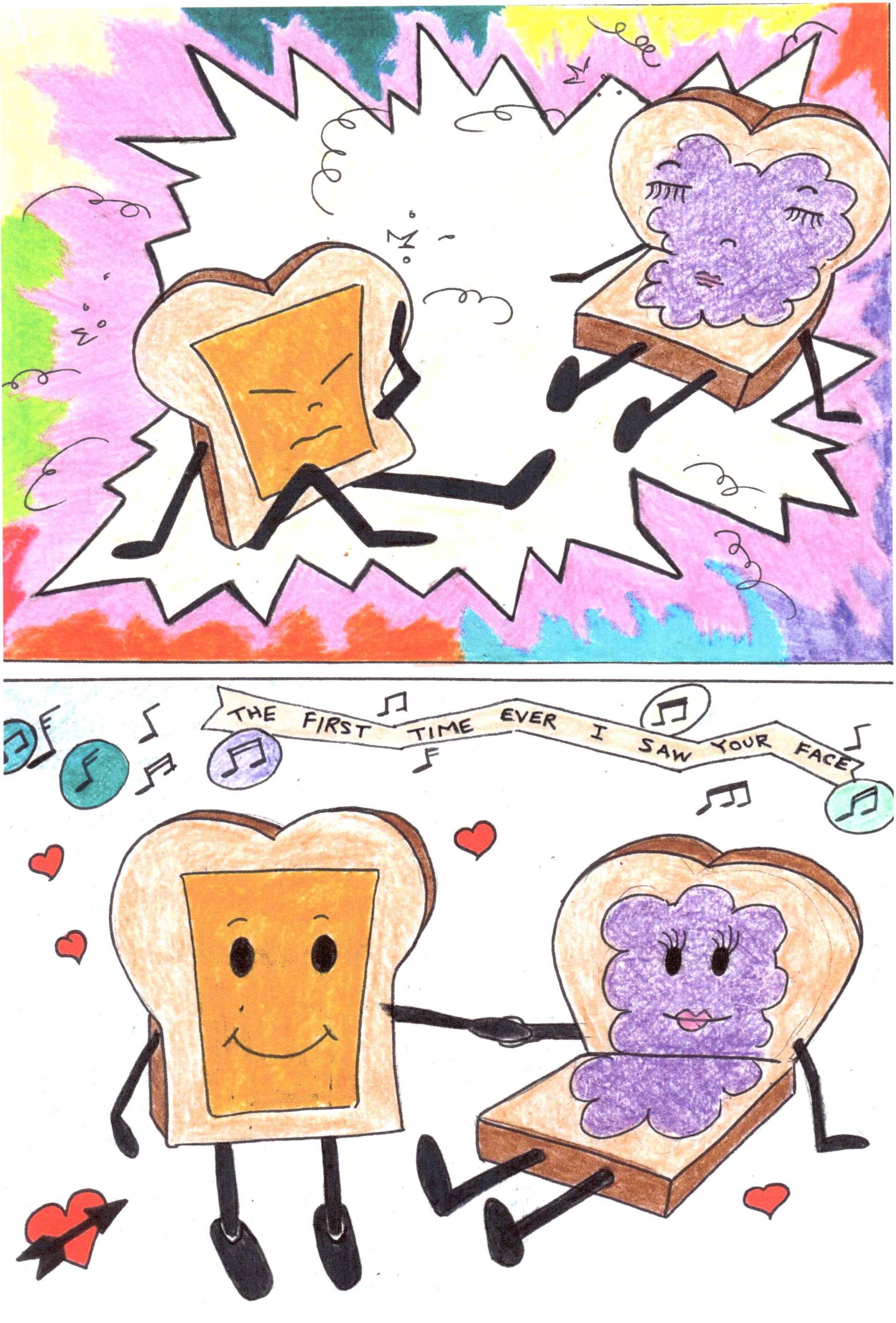

THE FIRST TIME EVER I SAW YOUR FACE

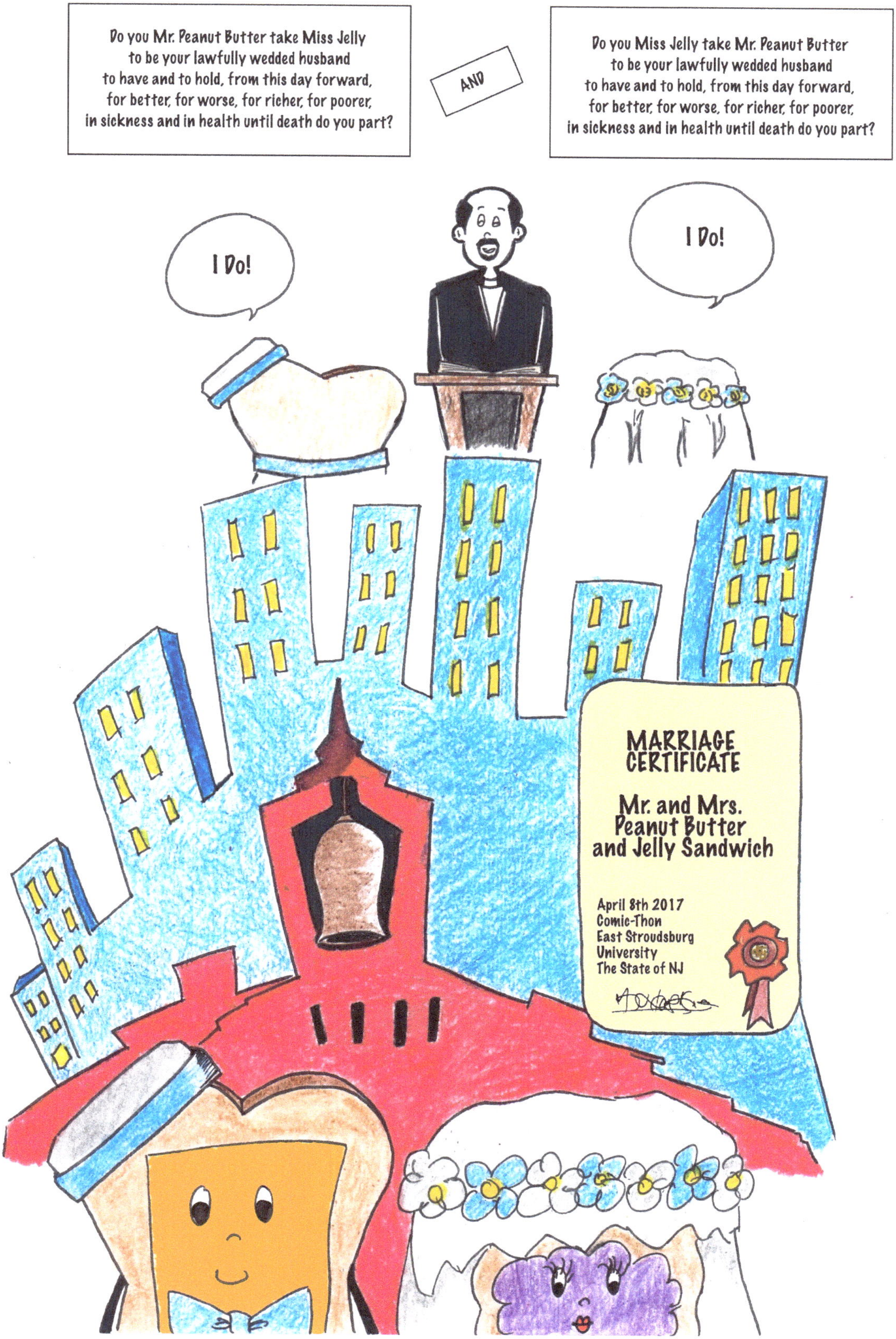

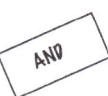

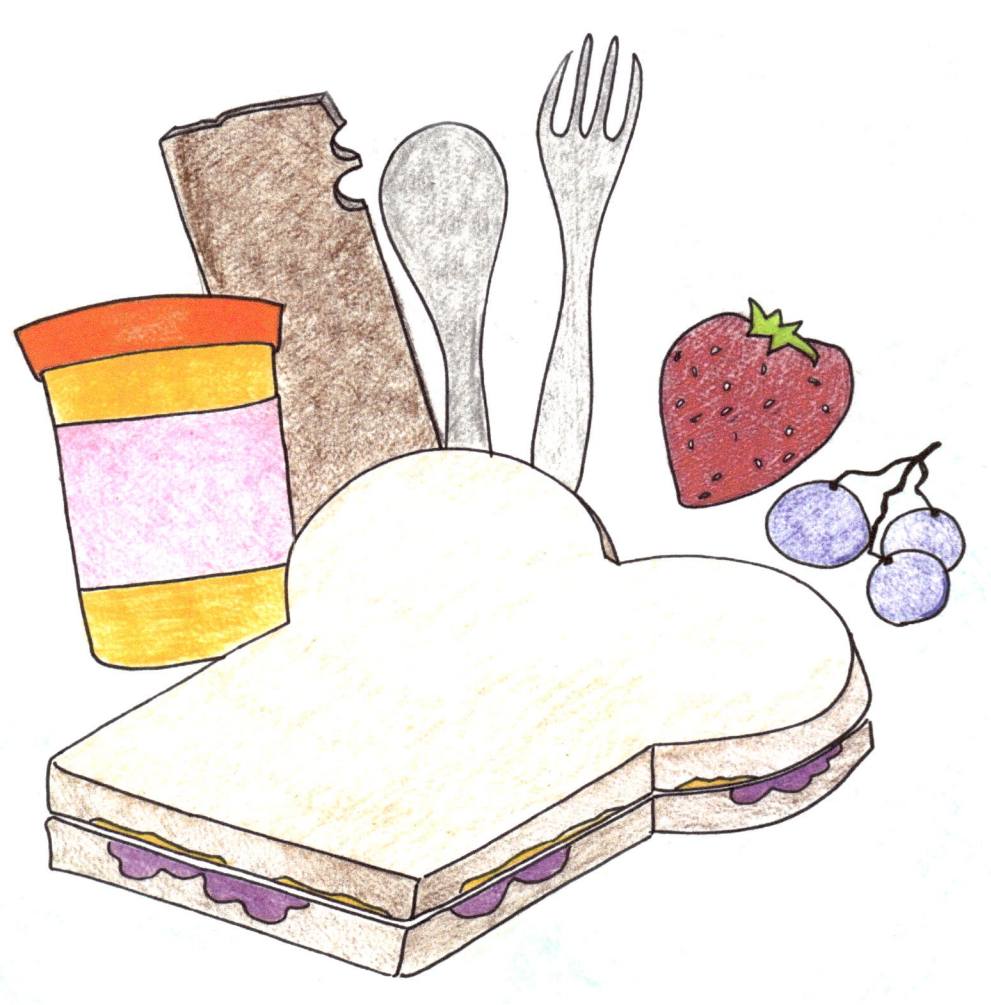

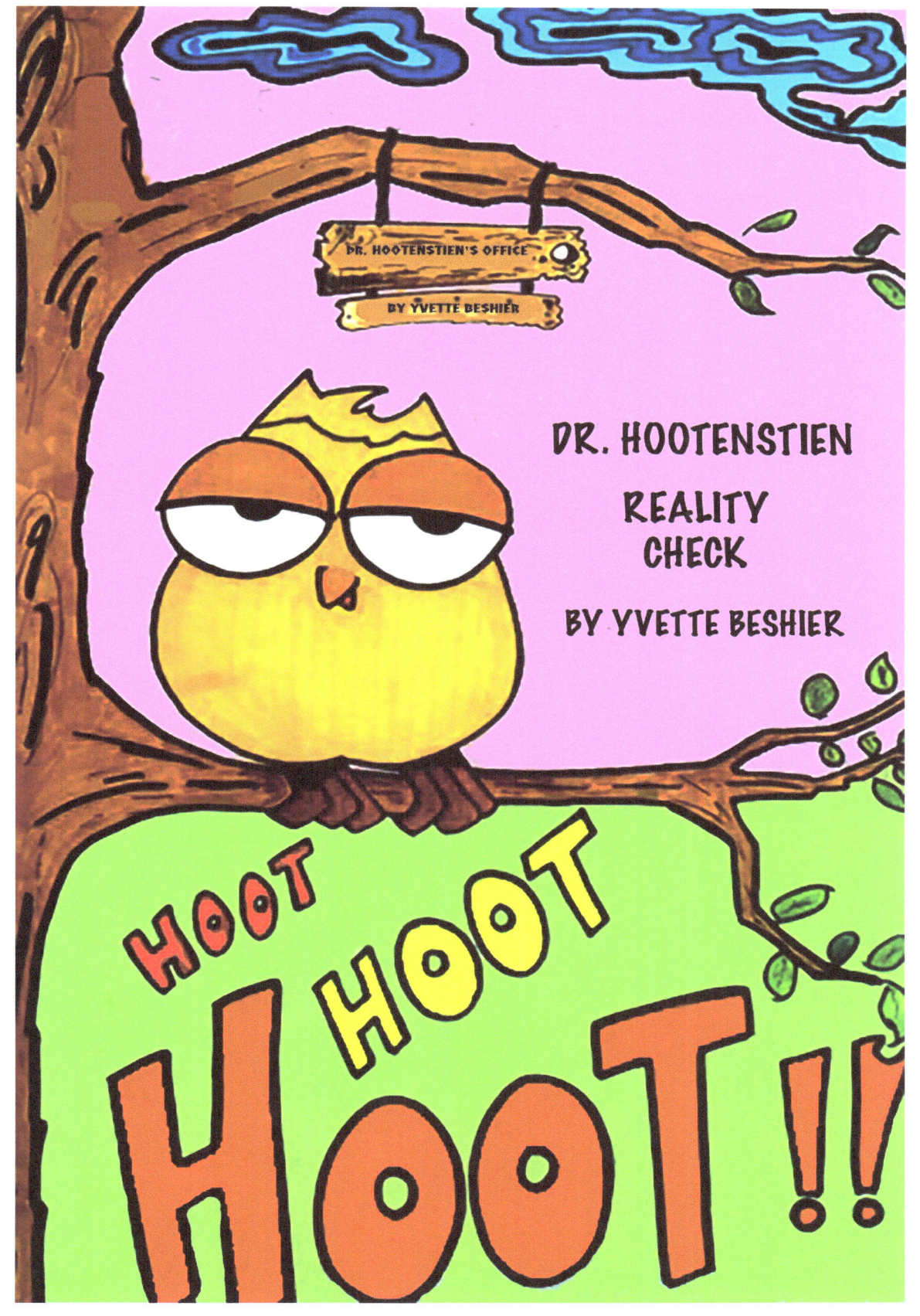

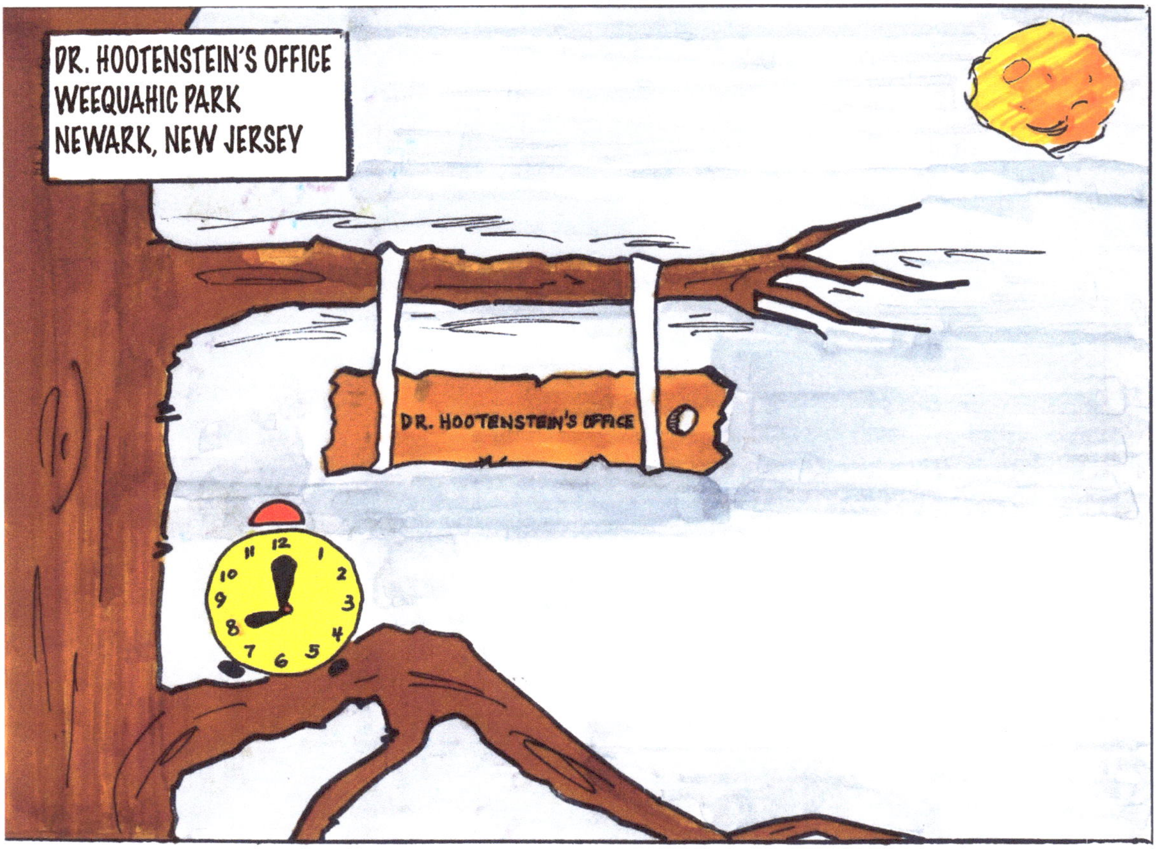

DR. HOOTENSTEIN'S OFFICE
WEEQUAHIC PARK
NEWARK, NEW JERSEY

DR. HOOTENSTEIN'S OFFICE

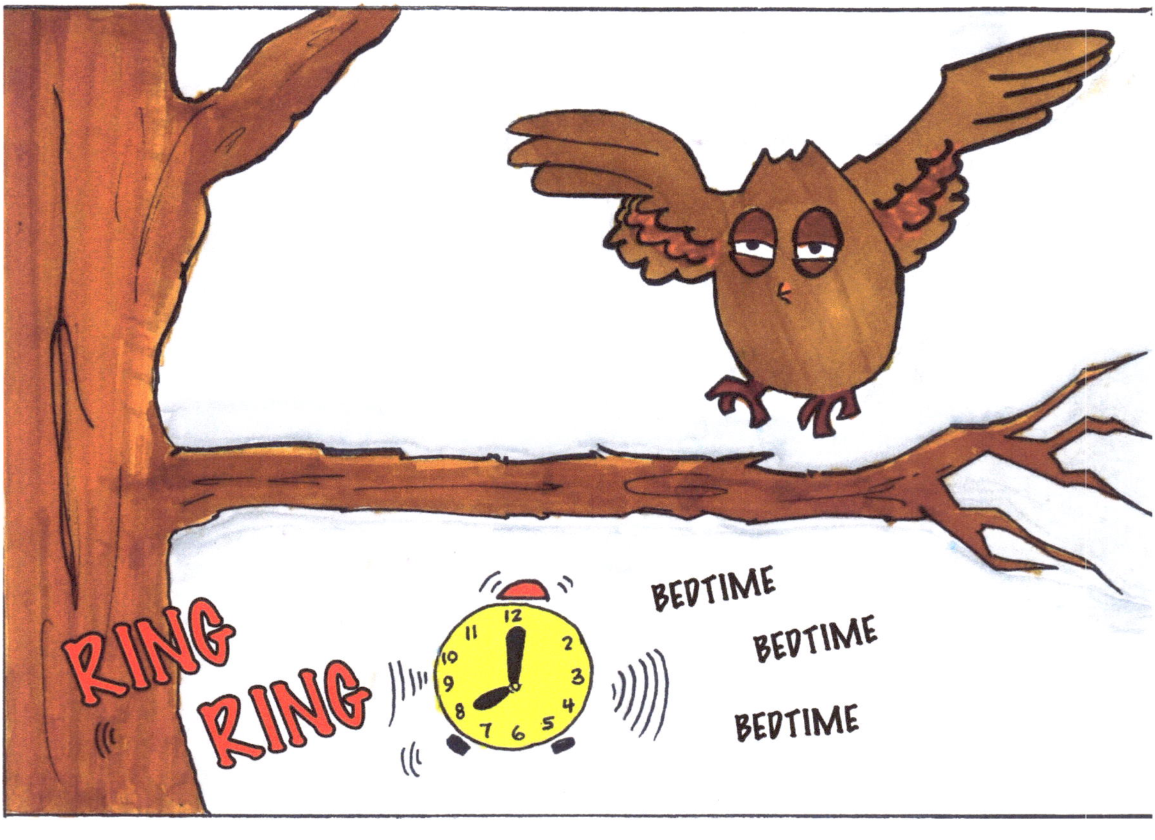

RING RING   BEDTIME
            BEDTIME
            BEDTIME

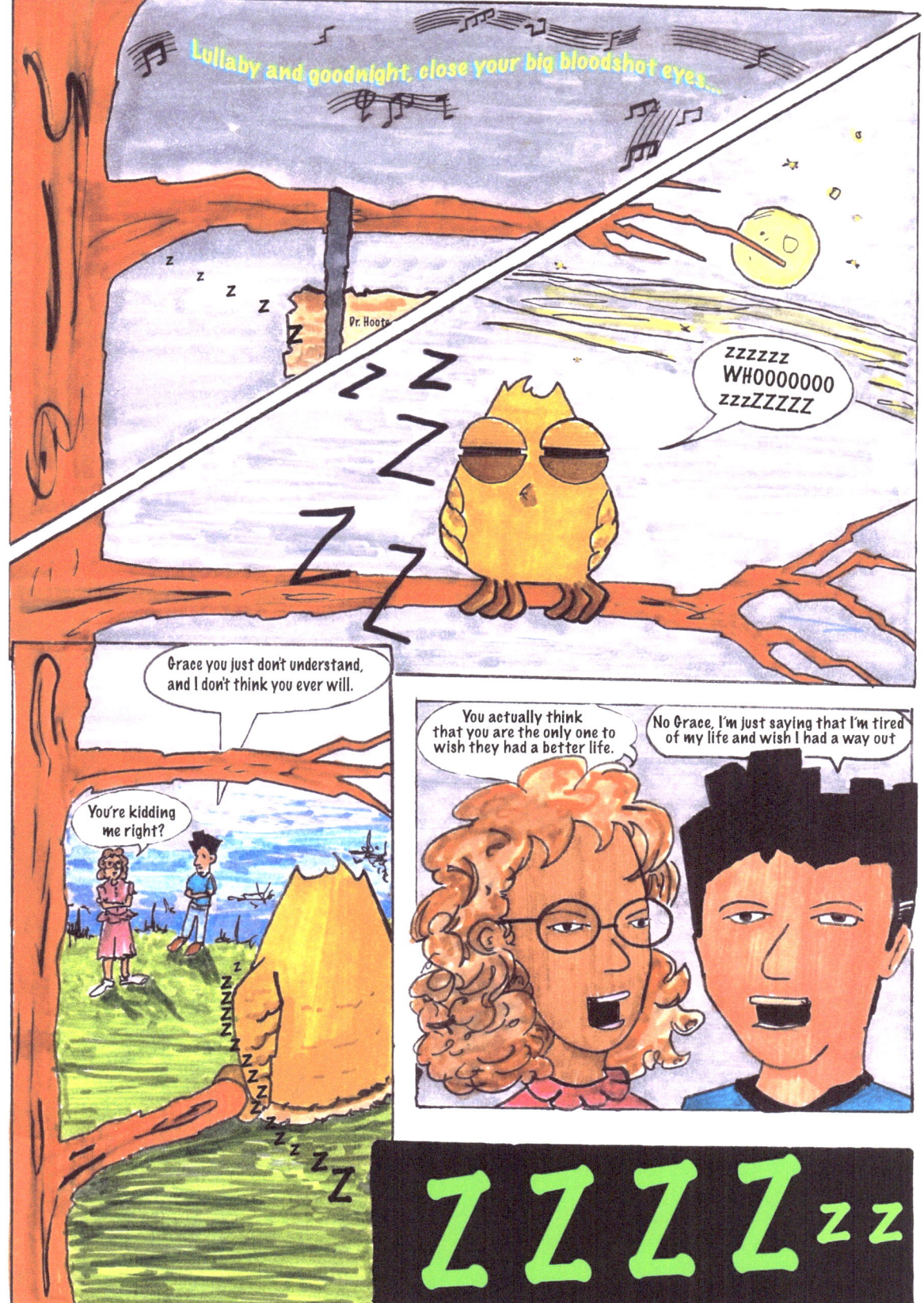

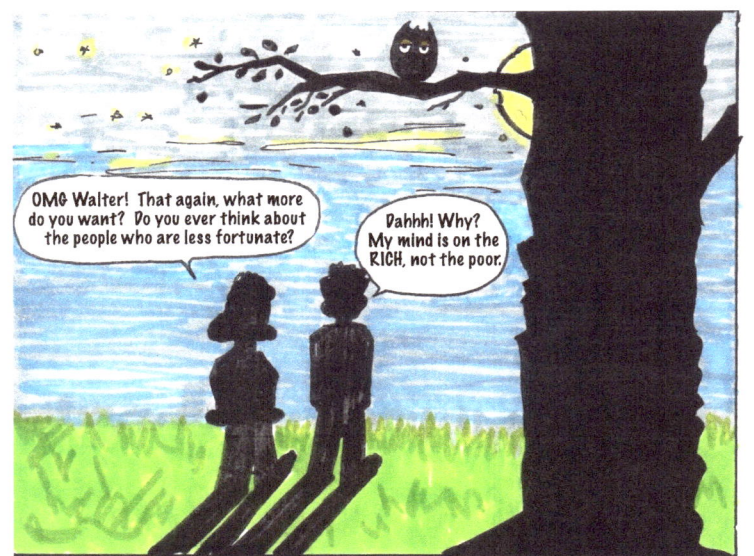
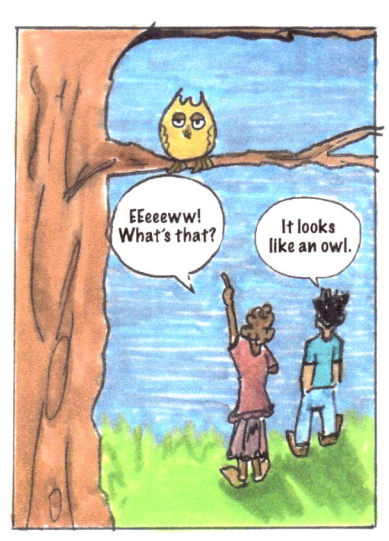

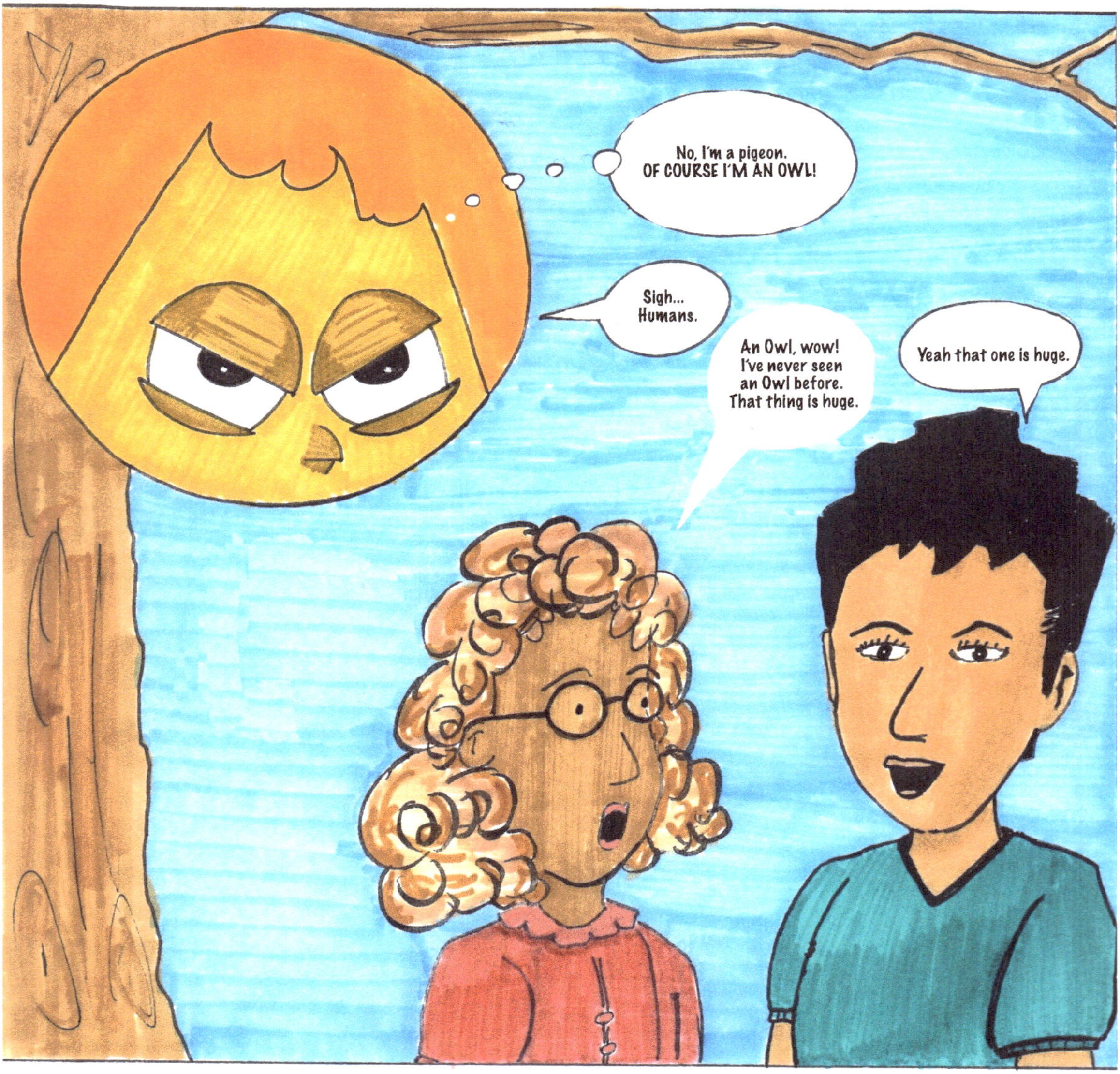

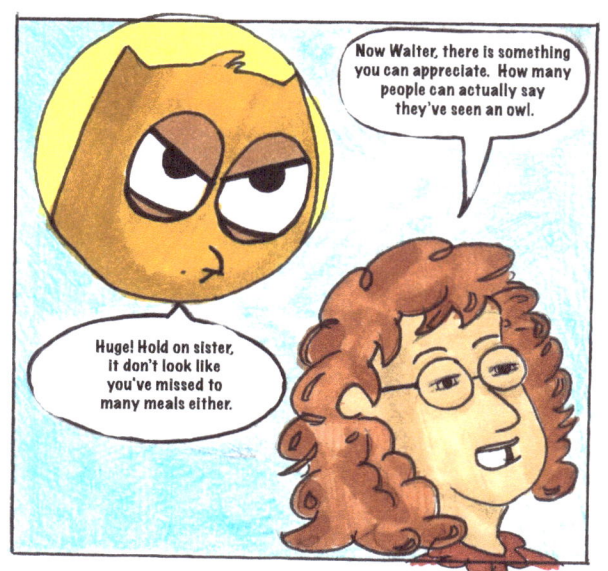
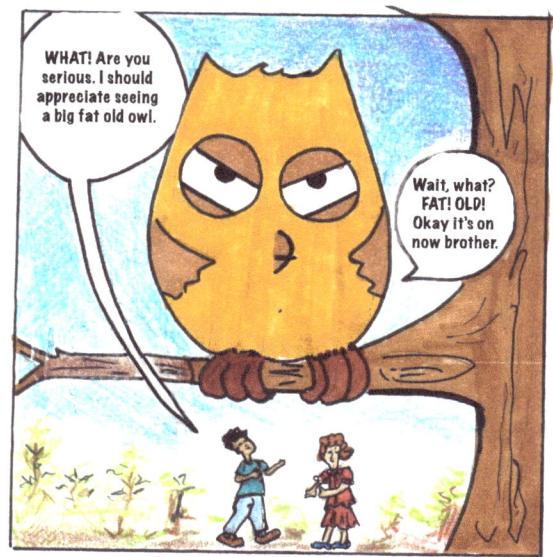
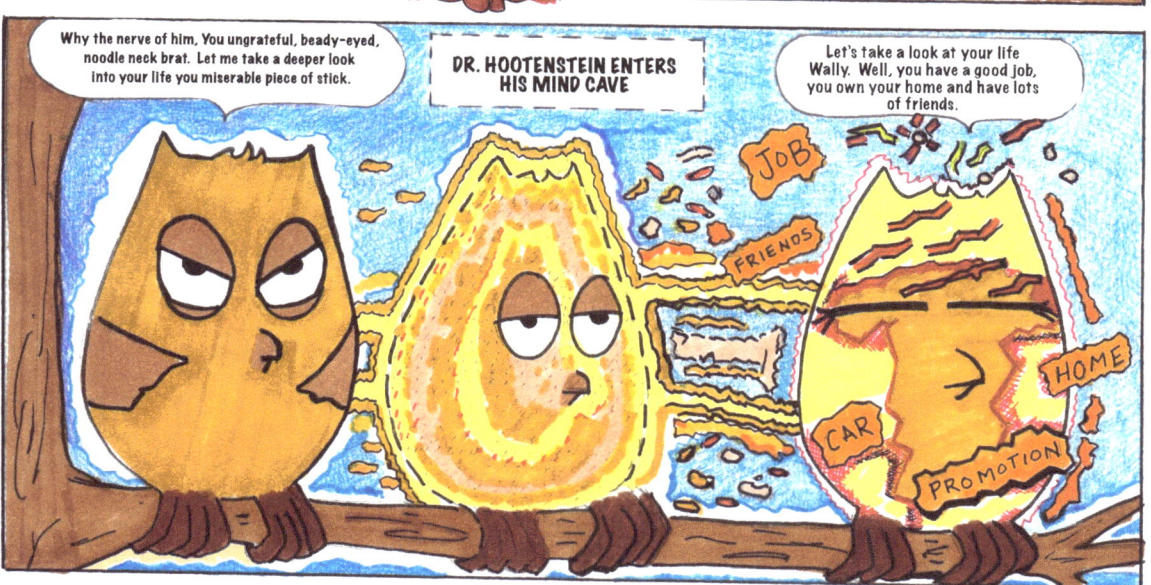
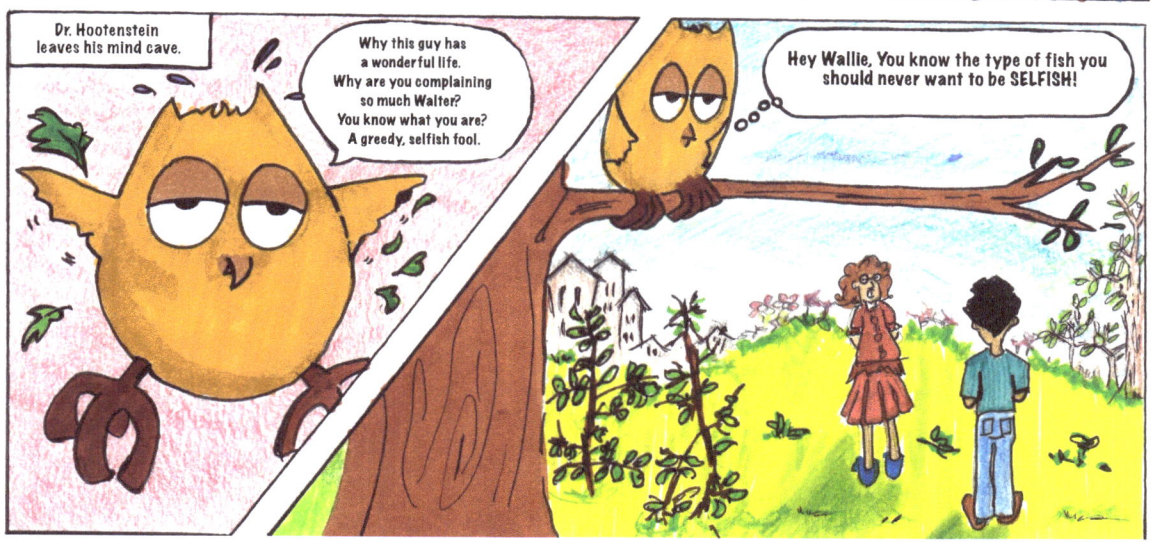

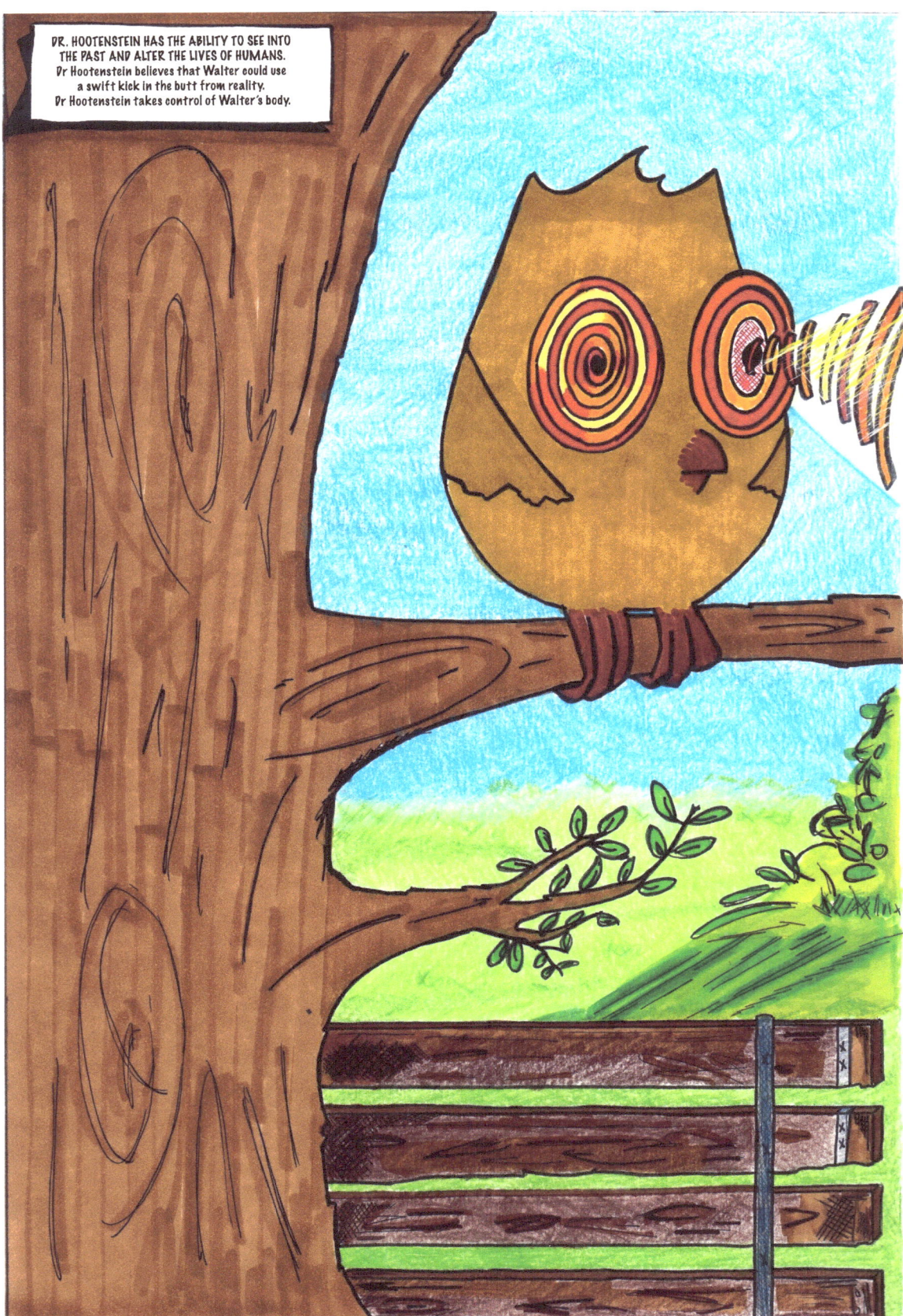

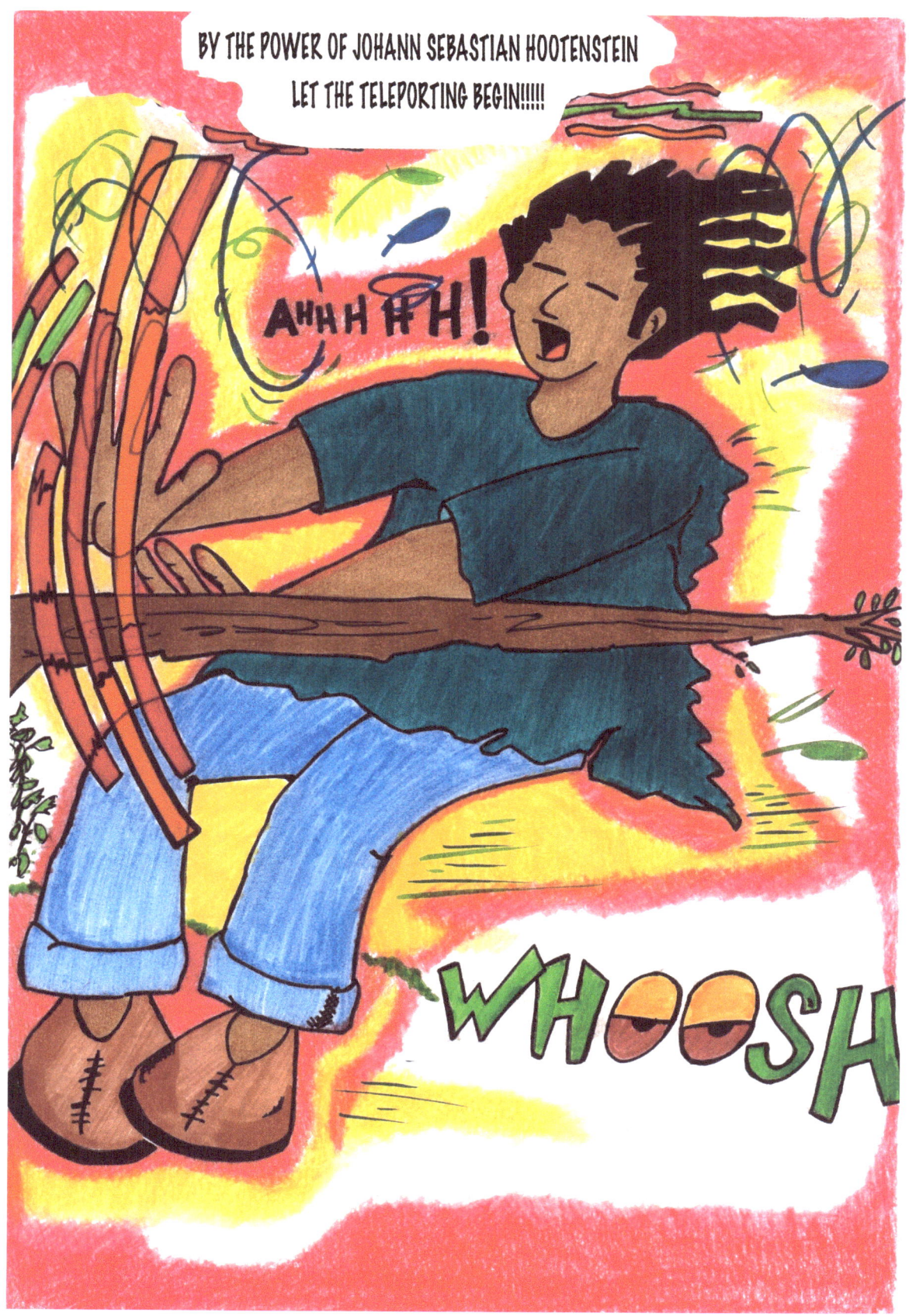

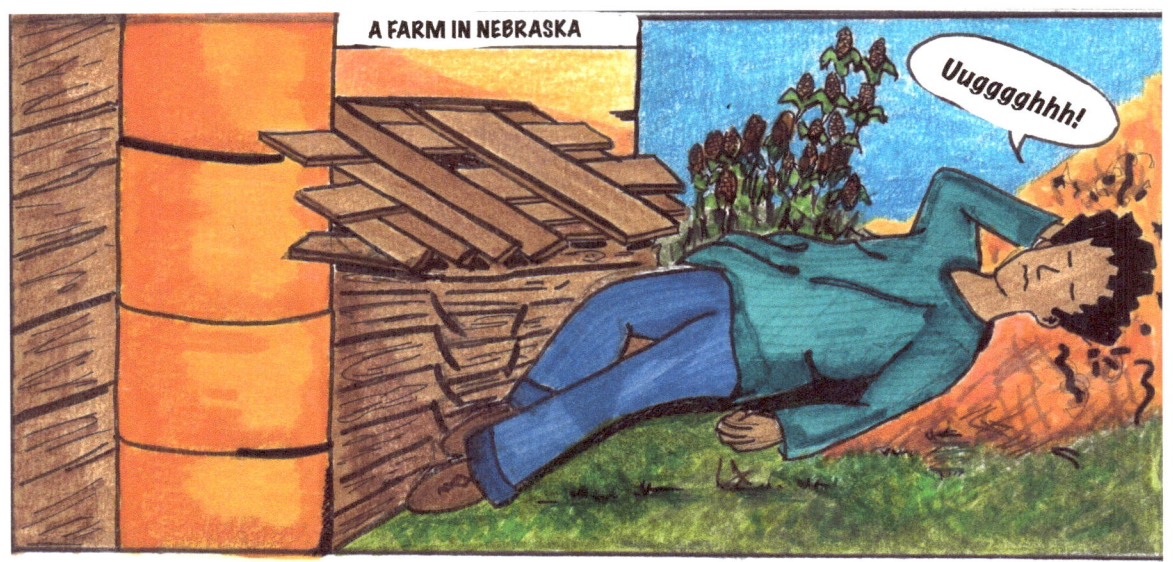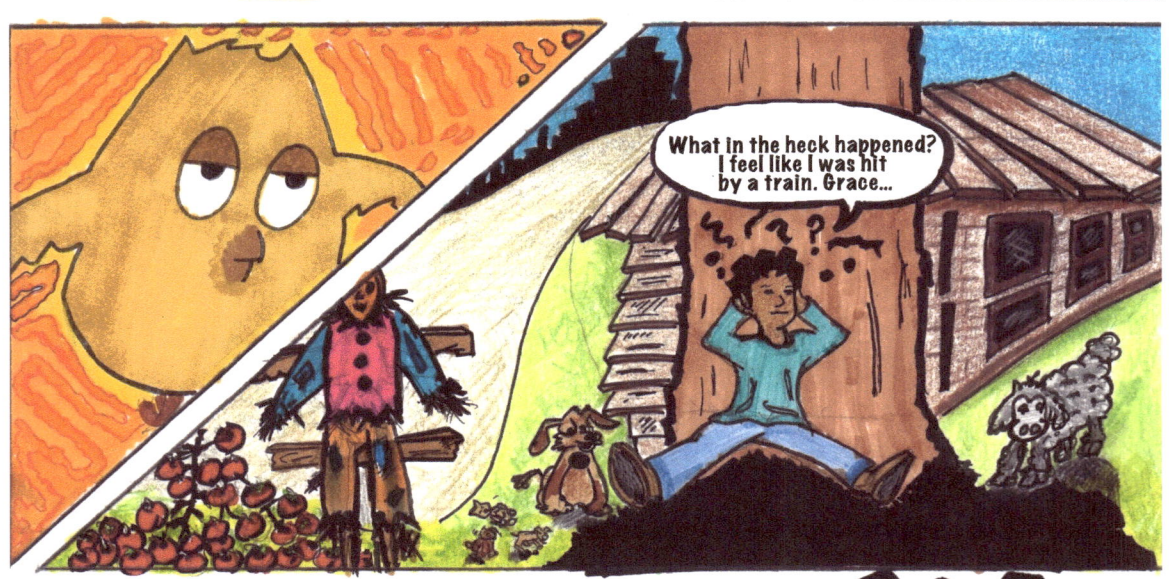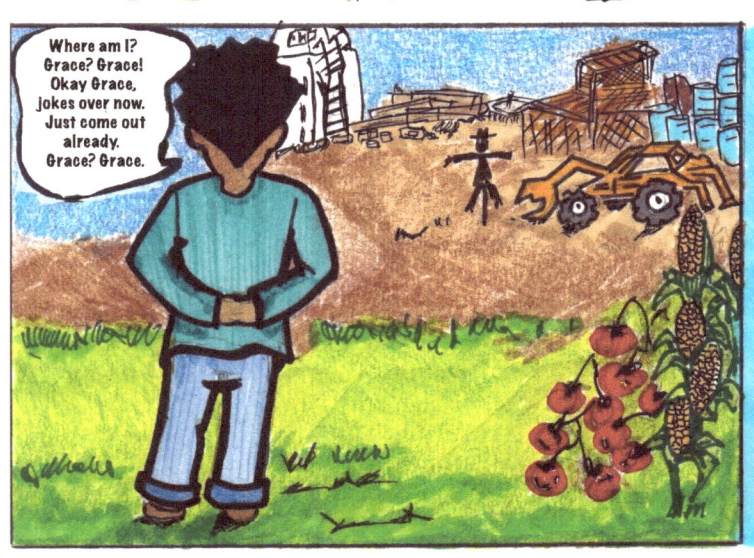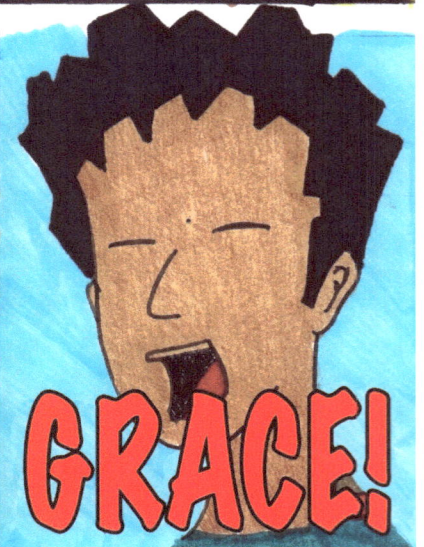

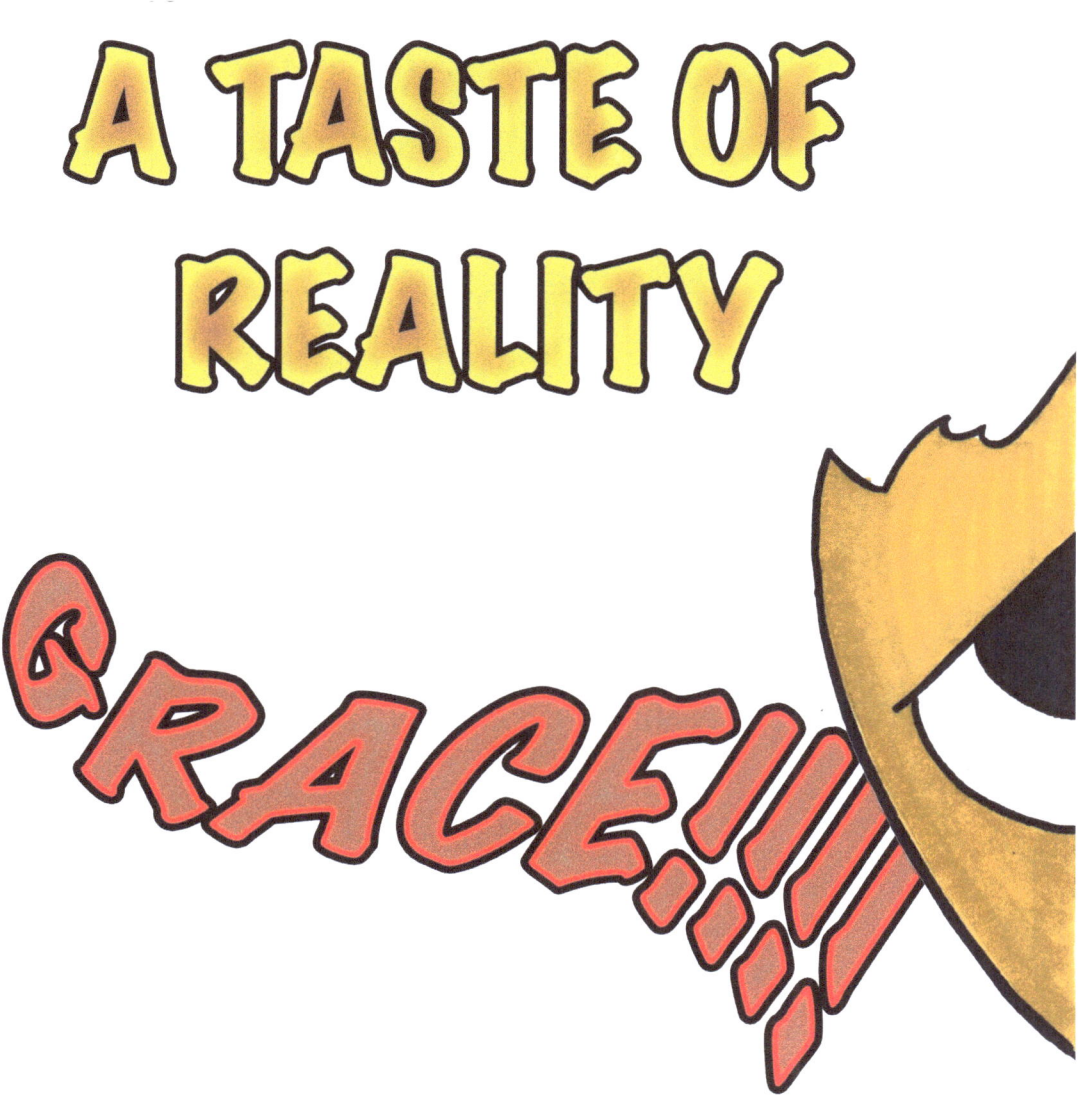

BONUS PIN-UPS

THE ADVENTURES OF NAYHAN AND NAMIR YOUNG RELIC HUNTERS

FEATURING: THE ROLO-BOTS

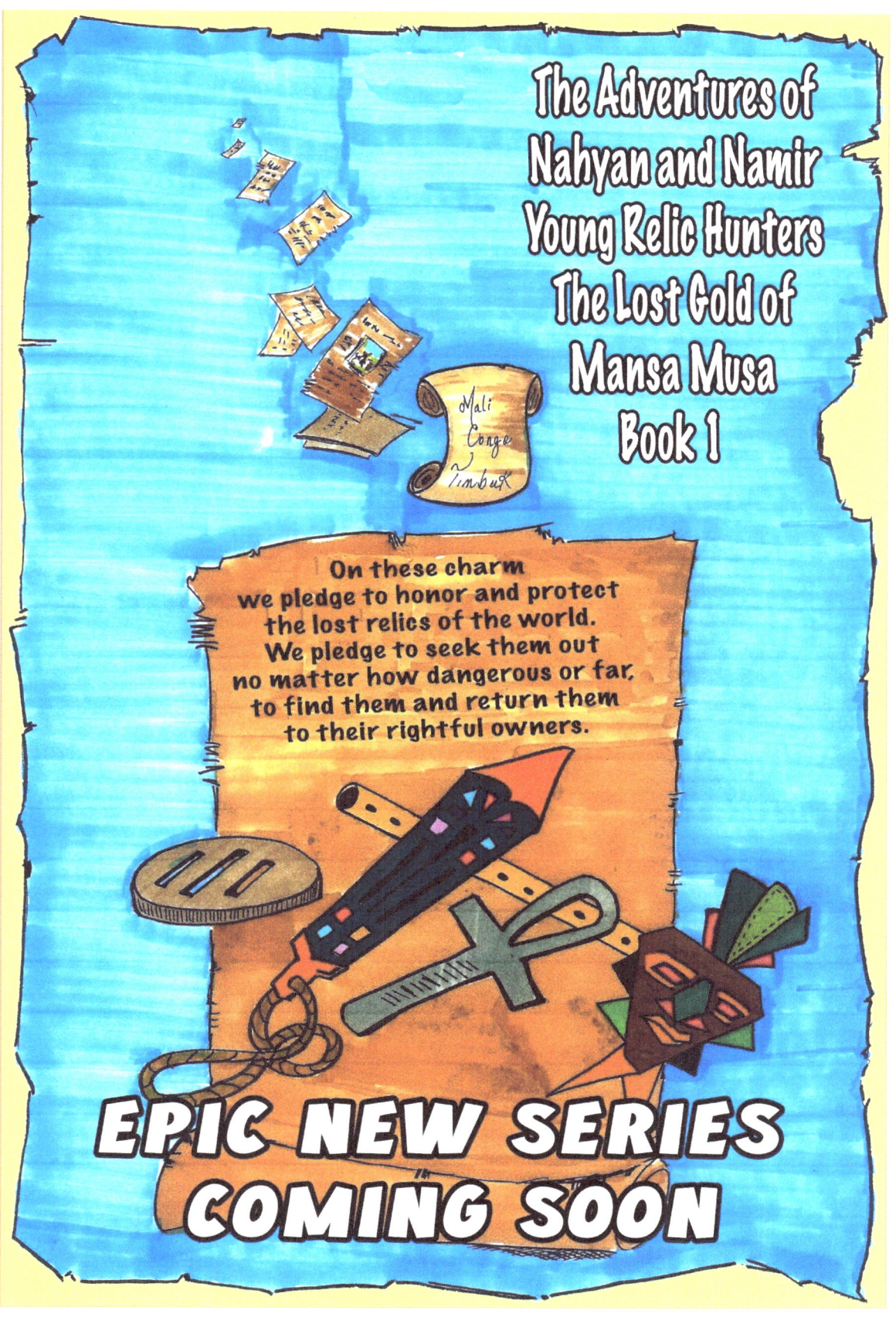

THE ROLOBOTS

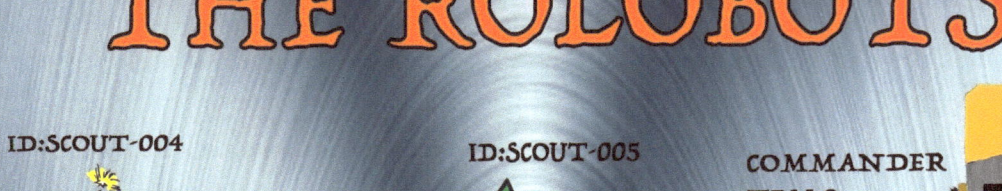
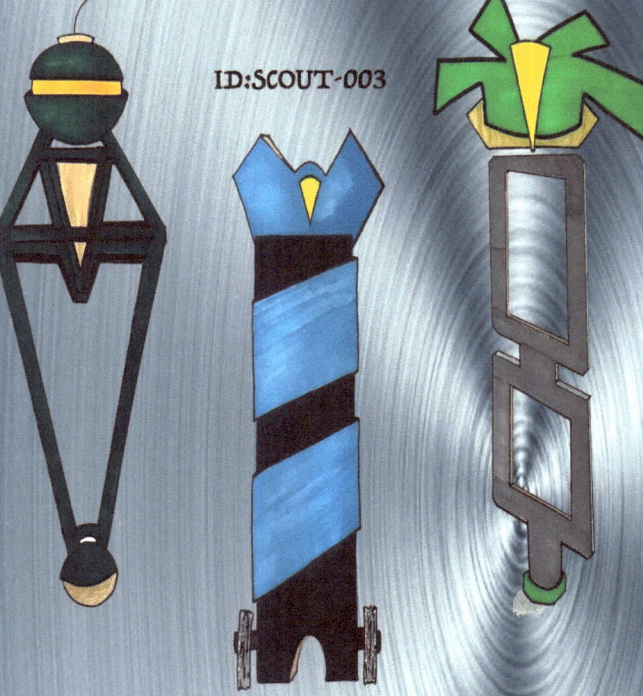
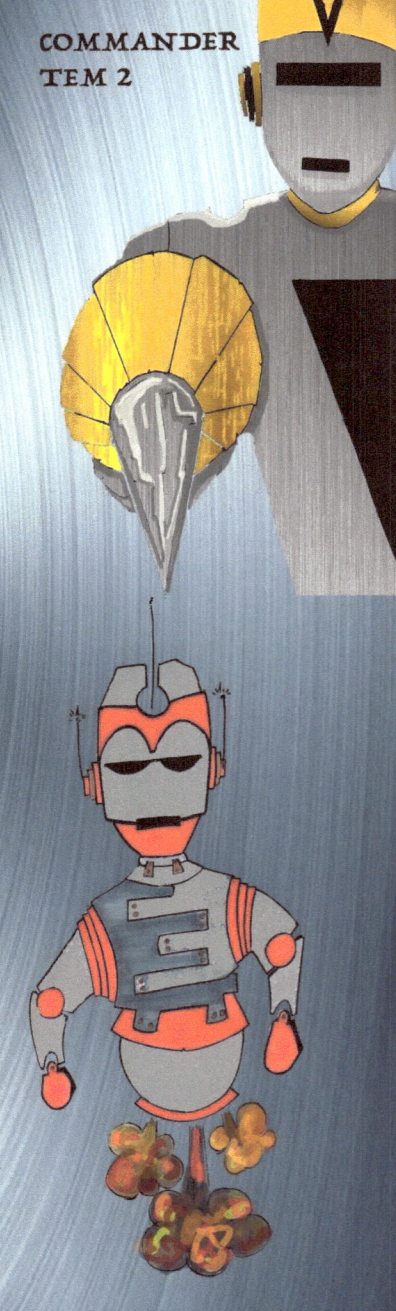
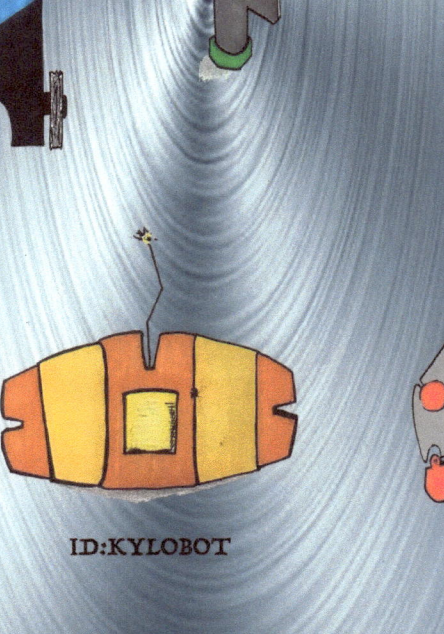
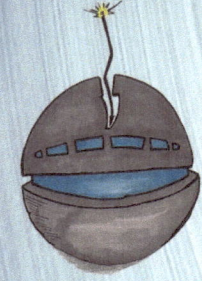

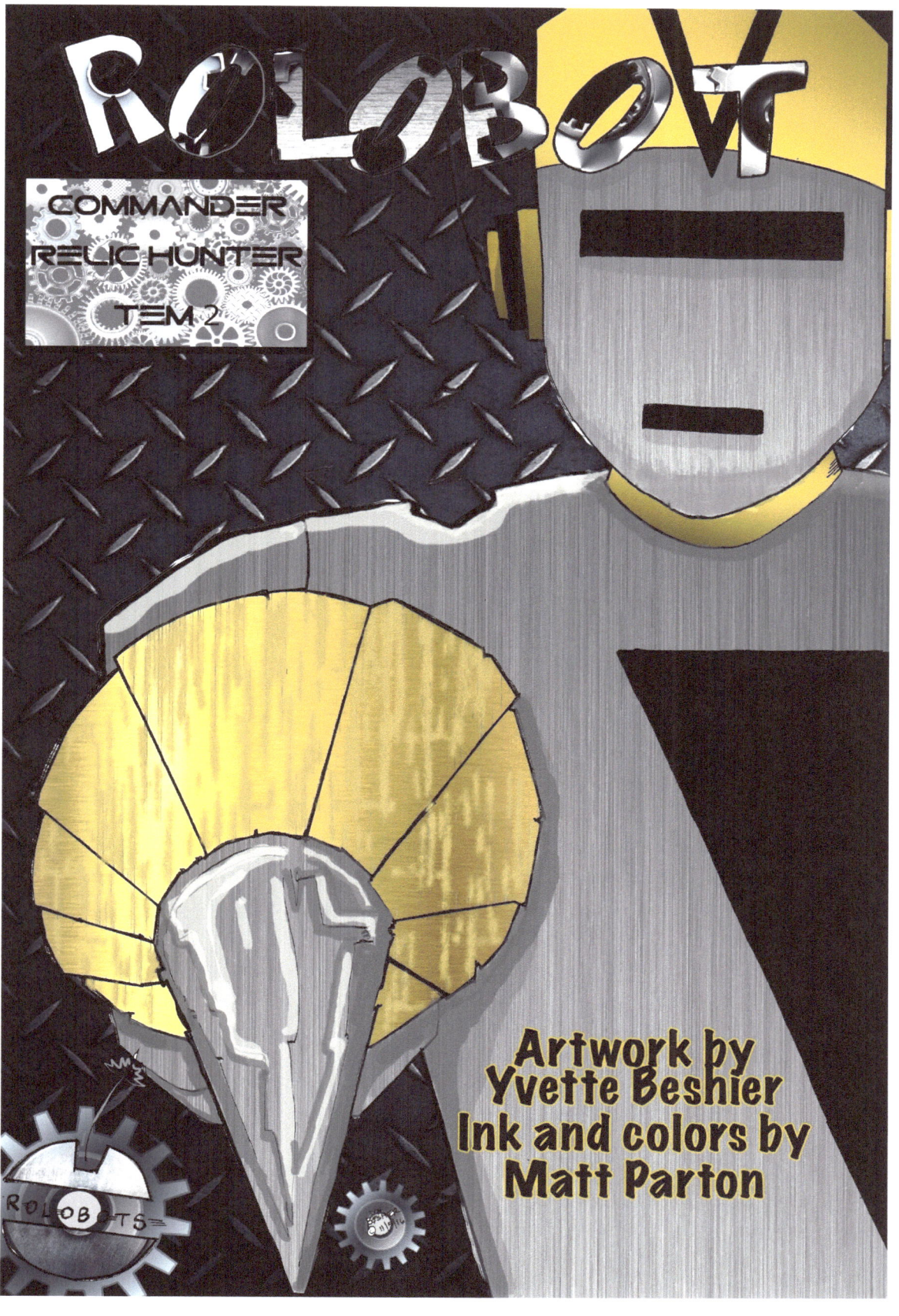

Yvette Beshier, LLC
yvettebeshier@aol.com

© 2012 Dr. Hootenstein - Reality Check
© 2016 How Peanut Butter Meet Jelly

All rights reserved. No portion of this book may be reproduced in any form without permission from the publisher, except as permitted by U.S. copyright law.

www.ingramcontent.com/pod-product-compliance
Lightning Source LLC
Chambersburg PA
CBHW042323250526
R18347300001B/R183473PG45473CBX00016B/7